Mothers, Mothering, and Sport

Experiences, Representations, Resistances

Edited by Judy Battaglia, Rebecca Jaremko
Bromwich, and Pamela Morgan Redela

DEMETER

Mothers, Mothering, and Sport:
Experiences, Representations, Resistances
Edited by Judy Battaglia, Rebecca Jaremko Bromwich,
and Pamela Morgan Redela

Demeter Press
140 Holland Street West
P. O. Box 13022
Bradford, ON L3Z 2Y5
Tel: (905) 775-9089
Email: info@demeterpress.org
Website: www.demeterpress.org

Demeter Press logo based on the sculpture "Demeter" by Maria-Luise Bodirsky
www.keramik-atelier.bodirsky.de

Printed and Bound in Canada

Front cover image, acrylic on canvas, Rebecca Jaremko Bromwich
Cover design and typesetting Michelle Pirovich

Library and Archives Canada Cataloguing in Publication
Mothers, mothering, and sport: experiences, representations, and resistances
/ edited by Judy Battaglia, Rebecca Jaremko Bromwich, Pamela Redela.
Includes bibliographical references.
ISBN 978-1-77258-170-6 (softcover)
1. Women athletes. 2. Mothers. 3. Motherhood. 4. Sports--Social aspects.
I. Battaglia, Judy, 1973-, editor II. Bromwich, Rebecca, 1976, editor III. Redela,
Pamela, 1975-, editor

MIX
Paper from
responsible sources
FSC® C004071

For everyone who plays,
and everyone who cheers them on:
may sports be a space of freedom,
where we can all take up a place.

Acknowledgments

We would like to acknowledge our home teams: we would be remiss if we did not expressly notice and express our gratitude for the profound importance of our children, spouses, and families to our work, and especially to recognize the support, mentorship, and empowerment we have been grateful to receive from Dr. Andrea O'Reilly and Demeter Press. You have made this work possible.

Contents

Introduction

Judy Battaglia, Rebecca Jaremko Bromwich,
and Pamela Morgan Redela

This anthology examines intersections between experiences of mothers, socially institutionalized expectations and discourses of mothering, and sport. These chapters cannot easily resolve this tension. Consequently, this anthology excavates a submerged space between what is compulsory and can be confining about the social imperative for middle class mothers to support their children's involvement in sports, and what can be transformative about mothers' participation in sport. This book offers a curated collection of chapters that present a repository of knowledges about how the work and identities characteristic of the social category "mother" connect with sport. Some of these knowledges are personal, some are subjugated, and some are more mainstream and academic.

This collection is both scholarly and personal. In putting together this book, we wondered what an interdisciplinary anthology focusing on motherhood and sport in the new millennium might look like, sound like, or feel like? What we have assembled is neither encyclopedic nor exhaustive; it is a starting point, an intervention of words to describe a myriad of rich, diverse, and intersectional experiences. We have combined creative and academic contributions; the authors whose contributions are featured in this text have written these chapters, and, in another sense, they *are* these stories. We hope this book helps to reimagine more emancipatory futures for mothers, mothering, and children, both inside and outside of the sporting context.

Mothers play a crucial role in supporting the sporting activities of their children (Lench). Although there is a growing field of feminist scholarship engaging with gender and sport (Scraton and Flintoff), this text makes a novel contribution to feminist scholarship about sport because it deals not only with women or gender as a category of analysis but with mothers as a social category distinct from, though related to, women. This work uniquely combines maternal feminist theory with feminist scholarship about sport. It emphasizes the key point that mothers' work in relation to sports is socially mandated. This collection focuses on motherhood as both an experience and institution, in the spirit of Adrienne Rich's *Of Woman Born* (1986). This anthology follows the theory of Andrea O'Reilly termed "matricentric feminism", that mother is a separate and distinct social category from that of woman. It also builds on the notion of "maternal thinking" theorized by Sara Ruddick (1989), and the related concept of motherwork.

This text offers contributions that critically inquire into how care for embodied subjectivity, understood as paradigmatically the work of mothers, connects to sport in practice, discourse, experience, and law. It also shows how the lived experiences of mothers and roles characteristic of mothering connect with the lived experiences of sport. The anthology also seeks to problematize how the ideology of intensive mothering—which imposes requirements on mothers to be primarily and centrally engaged in continuous efforts to nurture their children to the exclusion of pursuing their own interests or their careers (Hays)— intersects with the cultural imperative that mothers put their children into sports. A powerful mainstream North American cultural imperative exists that pushes mothers to spend their disposable income and time on supporting their children's activities in competitive sports. Mothers are expected to be "soccer moms," "football moms," "dance moms," and other hyphenated types of maternal supporters to child athletes. In this volume, such cultural pressure is highlighted and problematized by Helaina Bromwich's contribution, which narrates the pressure and stress felt by children to perform well.

The following chapters are written from various perspectives: artistic, autoethnographic, poetical, narratological, autobiographical, and historical-fictional. We use these various lenses to speak with the "both/and" nature of motherhood and sports, the plurality of voices that make up this subject, and the multivocality absent in books we ourselves wanted to read and teach on the subject.

These chapters explore family histories and familial lineages from a biological and psychosocial model of development, and from a performance studies perspective. Employing a critical-cultural lens, we look at what it means to play sport for leisure (i.e., is the love of the game truly only harboured in the amateur leagues now?), as well as explore pay for play politics, issues of intersectionality, neuroplasticity, the matrix of domination, coaching, motherhood, and pedagogy. We explore oral histories/herstories, and artistic pieces about representation and visibility, raising children through multiple linguistic lenses, motivation, and, most of all, consent. We do this in an attempt to illustrate and highlight the multiplicity of voices contained in motherhood, aunthood, and grandmotherhood, and to celebrate women in sport.

Included here are also stories of immigration and acculturation, as well as stories of struggle. Resilience and confidence are built through sport. It is an anti-Descartesian dualism for girls to experience sport with their bodies—a feeling of oneness absent in many other areas of their lives. Sport connects girls' bodies to their psyches and their spirits; it connects them to nature, parents, coaches, and peers. By having this text weave almost a revisionist herstory, perhaps we can help to undo some of the harmful effects other institutions (the media, the family, the state, religion, and sports) have laid upon women and girls today.

In the first chapter, "'We Changed Her Nappies. We Saw That She Was a Girl.' Caster Semenya's Femininity and the Power of Maternal Testimony," Celeste E. Orr and Amanda D. Watson look critically at the fact that C. Semenya's mother and grandmother are called upon to authenticate her sex and gender. They explore the way the women link the athlete's visible sex traits to her gender, and look at how this case reveals assumptions about sex and gender operating in the logics of sport, even though they have long been challenged by feminist and medico-scientific paradigms.

Kindell Foley Peters, in "Swim Coaches and Mothers: Exploring Pedagogy through Oral History," presents oral histories by female youth swim coaches, and explores how they relate to motherhood, mothers, and to coaching as pedagogy.

Catherine Ma, in "Quit Calling My Kid, Yao Ming: Reflections of Race and Class from a Chinese Basketball Mom" looks at how her experiences and knowledges as spectator, mother, psychologist, and researcher connect with race and class on the basketball court. The author looks critically at how her experience challenges and keeps static stereotypes of Asian and Asian American masculinity and its subsequent effects on mothering.

In "Ecofeminism Meets the Team Mom: Eco-Momma as Cultural Change Broker," Pamela Morgan Redela explores connections between environmental activism and the denigrated role of "team mom" as a heteronormative category subjugated to the stereotypically male role of coach. She looks at how "team mom" is constructed as an identity category in the consumer capitalist framework.

In "Concussions in Sport and Girls in Women's Rugby: Effectively Resisting and Moving beyond Confining Gender Norms and Mother-Blame: A Critical Discourse Analysis of the Rowan Stringer Case," Rebecca Bromwich explores how maternal agencies were deployed in successful law reform after the death of Ottawa teen rugby player Rowan Stringer. She looks at how through claiming the role of motherhood, activists, including Stringer's mother, were able to usher in new concussions legislation in Ontario. Her chapter investigates how sport and the maternal intersect to produce powerful spaces for girls and mothers to move and speak.

Last but not least, twelve-year-old Helaina Bromwich's personal narrative explores within competitive gymnastics the tension between cost, struggle, stress, strength, emancipatory power, and joy.

The relationship between mothering and mothers, and sport are multistranded, complex, and sometimes contradictory. Sport is seen as an emancipatory space for mothers, women, and children, yet it also contains elements from wider social interactions that are oppressive and unequal, and mandate the work of mothers. This book deliberately steps away from artificially resolving this profound and real tension. Although this anthology highlights the links between the ideology of intensive mothering and sport, it also argues that sport can be a liberatory space, where the constraints of gender and the social category of mother can be, to some degree, transformed and transcended by a different kind of physicality: a space where mothers and daughters can be warriors, and can enjoy their physicality for purposes other than the male gaze.

The generation of children born in the 1970s and 1980s, to which the editors of this volume belong, grew up with children's music that wasn't yet gendered–for example, campfire tunes, Raffi, Sharon, Lois and Bram, and Tom Chapin. We played the "Oregon Trail" on the first Apple computers, and had plenty of imaginary play such as the "Boat Game"—a game Judy engineered in which she and her friends were explorers and archeologists who were sent on a boat with a ration of food and they had to try and save animals and rescue precious artifacts and fossils. Pamela and her friends played at being pioneer women, such as Laura Ingalls from *Little House on the Prairie* or adventurous, physically strong detectives such as the women from *Charlie's Angels.* Rebecca remembers how much she cherished the simple freedom of riding her bike, and of playing softball with other girls, and the collaborative spirit of field hockey. It seemed a time and place (nostalgically, looking back) where girls could conquer adversity. We trusted our bodies to work by bike riding, skipping (often with linked arms), jumping rope, dancing, performing gymnastics, skating/blading, sledding, skiing, snowboarding, and doing other competitive and collaborative sports and games.

Notwithstanding decades of feminist scholarship and activism, our current moment as mothers living in the North-American, middle-class cultural mainstream is characterized by imperatives to conform to unmanageable expectations for our children's involvement in expensive, time-consuming sports and other activities, as well as by body shaming, self-consciousness, brand consciousness, and neoliberal capitalist consumerism. The contributions in this volume critically explore how sport may and may not provide mothers who are athletes, as well as mothers of athletes, with encouragement to take their rightful space as embodied subject in this world: whether that is physical space, sound space, visual space, virtual space, or simply a space in this anthology of women's voices. We hope to make these stories part of society's story, whether or not society is ready or willing to have them. We hope this anthology contributes to opening more space for mothers and athletes, and mothers as athletes, for all of us to experience life more freely. We envision alternative futures where mothers and children alike feel as unrestricted and uninhibited as we did when we were youngsters playing sports.

Works Cited

Lench, Brook, *Home Team Advantage: The Critical Role of Mothers in Youth Sports*. HarperCollins, 2006.

O'Reilly, Andrea, *Matricentric Feminism: Theory, Activism, Practice*. Demeter Press, 2016.

Rich, Adrienne. *Of Woman Born: Motherhood as Experience and Institution*. W. W. Norton, 1986.

Ruddick, Sara. *Maternal Thinking: Towards a Politics of Peace*. Beacon Press, 1989.

Scraton, Sheila, and Anne Flintoff. "Gender, Feminist Theory, and Sport." *A Companion to Sport*, edited by David Andrews and Ben Carrington, Wiley-Blackwell Publishing, 2013.

Chapter One

"We Changed Her Nappies. We Saw That She was a Girl."

Caster Semenya's Femininity and the Power of Maternal Testimony

Celeste E. Orr and Amanda D. Watson

In the 2011 television documentary *Too Fast to Be a Woman? The Story of Caster Semenya* (Ginnane), mother Dorcus Semenya and grandmother and primary caregiver Mmaphuthi Sekgala[1] discuss Caster Semenya's sex, gender, femininity, and sex-testing controversy. As in earlier media interviews, they remain resolute that the South African athlete is an authentic woman: they saw her genitals at birth and as they cared for her in infancy. Her body parts made her a woman, no matter her masculine characteristics.

Both the fact that C. Semenya's mother and grandmother are called upon to authenticate her sex and gender and the way the women link the athlete's visible sex traits to her gender reveal assumptions about sex and gender long challenged by feminist and medico-scientific paradigms. The women's testimonies centre on the apparent visual and dichotomous nature of sex and, consequently, fail to comply with apparently progressive and anti-interphobic[2] paradigms challenging normative views of sex as transparent and dichotomous (Fausto-Sterling; Jordan-Young; Oudshoorn; Karkazis, *Fixing Sex*; Davis; Kessler). In defending C. Semenya's womanhood, her mother and grandmother reinstate a sex and gender binary that many feminists across fields and cultures reject.

But to dismiss the testimonies of D. Semenya and Sekgala would be misguided, as they can also be read as challenging dominant tropes of femininity, women's sport, and so-called authentic womanhood. If C. Semenya can exhibit masculine traits and remain an authentic woman, as her mother and grandmother assert, femininity and masculinity are not so neatly tied to a sex binary. This reading nuances feminist sport literature condemning social pressure on women athletes to comply with rigid standards of feminine gender performance (Krane et al; Messner; Watson et al.). Reliance on the testimonies themselves also indicates, perhaps unexpectedly, some valuation of mothers and maternal knowledge by the mainstream media. In fact, we argue that examining these three readings together—the sex-gender binary, masculine women, and maternal knowledge—reveals the complex, intersecting power dynamics at play in the public scrutiny of C. Semenya and the treatment of D. Semenya and Sekgala as key informants.

We begin this chapter by situating C. Semenya's sex-testing controversy in the context of historical and contemporary sport sex testing. We then detail comments made by D. Semenya and Sekgala, and interpret them using relevant literatures on maternal knowledges (Nathoo and Ostry; Kelly and Radford; Apple; Wolf), colonial notions of African womanhood (Magubane, "Spectacles and Scholarship"; Munro; Gilman; McClintock), and intersex embodiments (Davis; Karkazis; Fausto-Sterling). Synthesizing these overlapping literatures to interpret the mothers' comments featured in the documentary, we resist the idea that D. Semenya's and Sekgala's narratives about sex are interphobic and, therefore, backward and antiscience (Magubane). Instead, we argue that the mothers' testimonies must be read against the backdrop of colonization, imperialism, biological racism, determinism, and essentialism, which positions African women, particularly South African women, as naturally sexually ambiguous. Failing to attend to their narratives reflects how maternal knowledge is frequently undermined (Kelly and Radford)—which would be particularly regrettable, as their testimonies effectively expand the confines of femininity and, in doing so, challenge the dominant ethos that so-called authentic femininity is frail, unmuscular, less athletic, thin, and white (Collins).

Controversy and Sport Sex Testing

C. Semenya was subjected to sex testing in 2009 after her victory at the Berlin Games. Her test results were not officially made public. However, speaking about C. Semenya on 20 August 2009, International Association of Athletics Federations (IAAF) spokesperson Nick Davies claimed, "It's [C. Semenya's embodiment] seen as a medical condition" (Ginnane; Davies qtd. in Jamieson). Even though no official documents were made public, "certain very detailed claims were leaked" (Hoad 401), which prompted international news sources—including the UK's *Telegraph* (Hart), New York's *Daily Telegraph* (Hurst), and Sydney's *Daily News* (Yaniv)—to publish intimate details about her body. In this moment, various sources effectively imposed intersex status as both a pathological diagnosis and an identity onto C. Semenya (Munro), a status that she has never claimed (Brady 4; Magubane, "Spectacles and Scholarship" 762).

Sport sex testing is thought to ensure a level playing field. Women athletes are tested, presumably to protect them from the ostensibly "unfairly advantaged 'hermaphrodites' who regularly defeated 'normal women'" (Cahn 111). Testing is intended to detect unfairly advantaged female athletes with intersex traits or, in pathological terms, disorders of sex development (DSD)—primarily hyperandrogenism, which is characterized by naturally high levels of androgens, such as testosterone. Supporters of sex testing maintain that testosterone is not only a marker of one's true sex but also a marker of one's unfair athletic capabilities (Tucker).

This basic premise is misinformed. As Rebecca Jordan-Young and Katrina Karkazis verify referencing Joe Leigh Simpson et al.'s 2000 study, "testosterone is not the master molecule of athleticism. One glaring clue is that women whose tissues do not respond to testosterone at all are actually overrepresented among elite athletes. As counterintuitive as it might seem, there is no evidence that successful athletes have higher testosterone levels than less successful ones." There is also no conclusive evidence to suggest that athletic abilities are purely a matter of, or exclusively extend from, sex, however sex is defined (Dworkin and Cooky; Zaccone; Kane; Karkazis and Jordan-Young).

Moreover, the idea of a level play field is untenable. Numerous studies and scholars demonstrate that sport has never been, and never could be, entirely fair (Cooky and Dworkin; Zaccone; Sage; McDonagh and Pappano; Buzuvis; Messner; Camporesi and Maugeri). As Cheryl Cooky and Shari L. Dworkin explicate, "sport as a level playing field is neither an organizational reality nor a possibility, given the historical and contemporary social, economic, and cultural arrangements of sport" (107). Moreover, committees do not and cannot police all of the "myriad physical advantages that are not available to nor attainable by all athletes" (Cooky and Dworkin 107). Such physical advantages include extreme tallness (diagnosed as acromegaly) (e.g., Kenny George), a long wingspan, (e.g., Michael Phelps [Cooper]), or increased hemoglobin levels and oxygen capacity (diagnosed as congenital polycythemia) (e.g., Ero Mäntyranta [Cooky and Dworkin]). Yet the idea of a woman being advantaged by her sex characteristics remains disconcerting to sport federations (e.g. IAAF, International Olympic Committee [IOC]) and viewers (Watson et al.). This institutional preoccupation with women's sexual anatomy in sport suggests we are more concerned with the maintenance of a sex and gender binary—in which men are deemed naturally more competent than women and, therefore, disinclined to be deceitful regarding gender—than we are with physical characteristics that advantage athletes by other means. As sports citizenship scholars have noted, this anxiety about women athletes, particularly women athletes with (suspect) intersex traits, is not about fairness (Sykes; Travers; Watson et al.). In fact, policing gender and sex segregation in sport reinforces male supremacy and heteronormativity with terrible consequences for women and people with intersex traits, which extend beyond the arena of sport (Travers). We would not expect athletes with webbed feet or very large wingspans to undergo surgery to reverse or fix these biological traits, but we see women athletes expected to undergo irreversible hormone therapy or even surgery to reduce traits correlated with masculinity (Jordan-Young et al.).

Many studies illuminate how sex testing promotes and relies on interphobia, cissexism (Cavanagh and Sykes), Eurocentric notions of femininity (Pieper), and the false belief that sex is objectively definable and dichotomous (Daston and Galison; Jordan-Young; Jordan-Young and Karkazis, *Fixing Sex*; Laqueur; Oudshoorn; Hird; Herdt; Fausto-Sterling, *Sexing the Body*). Sex testing is also critiqued because it is not uniform, and this lack of uniformity reveals the sexist ideologies underpinning the practice (Cooky and Dworkin; Dworkin and Cooky;

Travers; Cahn). For instance, only women were historically tested; now, only women who allegedly appear too muscular, too masculine, or are too athletically capable raise suspicion (Cooper 235; Karkazis, "The Ignorance"; Pieper, "Sex Testing"). In other words, women who excel in sport and do not conform to sexist, interphobic, and cissexist standards of femininity, and feminine beauty are suspected to be not real women.

Meanwhile, male athletes never provoke such outrage. They are never questioned or tested because "all men in sport are assumed to be 'real men' at the outset" (Dworkin and Cooky 21). Men are expected to be capable, athletic, and muscular. It is clear that sex tests function to maintain "one of the most central and coveted beliefs in sport"—namely, men have inherently superior athletic capabilities and bodies compared to women (Dworkin and Cooky 21; Cooper; Kane). Or, in Vikki Krane's terms, "[t]he underlying message is that athleticism and femininity are contradictory" (115). Athleticism and femininity are understood to be, and are represented as, antithetical. This discriminatory idea is then institutionalized by IAAF and IOC sex-testing policy.

Sex testing is also not uniform across race and nation, as women of colour from colonized nations in the Global South are targeted for sex testing (Mitra; Davis, 152; Karkazis, "The Ignorance"). As Jennifer Hargreaves and Tavia Nyong'o (2010), among others (Cooky et al.; Pieper), confirm: sex testing is informed by intersecting racist and sexist ideologies that have colonial roots (Magubane; Munro; Hoad). Patricia Hill Collins's insights are instructive on how white supremacist racial logics play out in sex and gender suspicion. She explains that Black women "by definition, cannot achieve the idealized feminine ideal because the fact of Blackness excludes them" (Collins 99). Idealized femininity is white (Kilbourne; Deliovsky). Embodying hegemonic femininity, thus, involves gender conformity as well as looking, being, or passing as white (Collins 193). Black women—and women of colour in general—are thereby excluded from authentic womanhood, and are always and already under suspicion (Pieper; Somerville).

Given these intersecting ideologies, C. Semenya's Blackness, muscular body, "unfeminine" gender presentation, and remarkable athletic abilities render her intensely suspect. Her body and capabilities challenge and threaten views about what women look like and are capable of doing. Questioning her womanhood through sex testing is a means to (re)stabilize hegemonic white femininity and serves to (re) emphasize the notion that Black women are not real women. In the documentary about the controversy, C. Semenya challenges hegemonic femininity by asking, "What makes a lady? Does it mean if you're wearing skirts and dresses you're a lady? No. What kind of a lady is that? Yeah I'm a lady. There's nothing I can say, yes, I'm a lady. I have those cards of being a lady" (Ginnane). C. Semenya's comments reveal the incoherence of a patriarchal culture that demands the accoutrements of feminine performance from women while, at the same time, devaluing femininity and women as materialistic, superficial, and incompetent. Dee Amy-Chinn describes the "core femininity" required of athletes—"appropriate dress, adornment, deportment and interest in things 'girly' (notably clothes and shopping)" (315)—which starkly contrasts the physical expectations of sport, especially for large, muscular women athletes (Krane et al.). It is not a stretch to imagine how, in this context, Semenya is deemed responsible for her own sex test surveillance because she refuses legible feminine performance (Butler) in the form of compliant comportment and matching nail polish to a bikini uniform.

In 1991, the IAAF stopped sex testing all women athletes because of complaints about the humiliating nature of the tests and mounting evidence that sex cannot be reduced to chromosomes and sex is not objectively definable or dichotomous (de la Chapelle; Cooper; Dworkin and Cooky; Donnellan). In 2000, the IOC followed suit. However, the IOC and IAAF retained "the right to examine female athletes that raise suspicion" (qtd. in Cooper 247) and treat women who fail examinations accordingly. C. Semenya, among others, raised enough suspicion.[3]

Too Fast to Be a Woman?

In 2009, as tests were underway and C. Semenya was banned from competing, *Too Fast to Be a Woman?* filmmakers were given "unprecedented access [to C. Semenya's situation] during the most testing period of her life as she fought to run again" (Ginnane). In addition to documenting C. Semenya's story of violence and exclusion from competition, her lawyer's trials, and various statements made by experts and IAAF representatives, the filmmakers include commentary from her mother and grandmother, D. Semenya and Sekgala, about C. Semenya's sex and womanhood. At the time, D. Semenya's and

Sekgala's testimonies were prominently featured in various news outlets—the *Guardian* ("Caster Semenya's Mother"), the *New Yorker* (Levy), the *Telegraph* ("Mother of 800m Winner"), among others (Dixon; "My Child Is Not a Man"; "Mother Insists"). The mothers were questioned in search of the truth about C. Semenya's sex, which was constructed around their authentications. In the documentary, D. Semenya and Sekgala remain resolute that C. Semenya is an authentic woman because they saw her genitals at birth and as they cared for her in infancy. "It [the sex testing controversy] never went to my head," Sekgala explains, "she [C. Semenya] was born in front of us. We changed her nappies. We saw that she was a girl" (Ginnane). Likewise, D. Semenya clarifies, "when they started saying she's not a girl, she's a boy, I never had a problem. I gave birth to her and, as a mother, know that she's a girl not a boy" (Ginnane).

The fact that their comments became important reflects a dual assumption: sex and gender are visual and mothers must have privileged knowledge about the sex and gender of the children for whom they care. In a moment, we expand upon the latter to consider the position of mothers represented here. We first turn to assumptions about the visual nature of sex and gender. D. Semenya and Sekgala draw from the hetero/cisnormative and interphobic commonsense narrative that looking at one's genitals reveals and confirms one's sex and, therefore, gender. They saw C. Semenya's genitals and confirmed that she was a girl and would grow up to be a woman, no matter what typically masculine characteristics or abilities she possessed. Their testimonies are intended to confirm that C. Semenya has "legible genitals" (Karkazis, *Fixing Sex* 95), that she was not born with "variant genitals" (Kessler 34), and that she was not "sexless" but readily "sexable" (Preves 52).[4] According to this account, her genitals signify her innate femininity. D. Semenya continues as follows:

God has made this family to be one blood; we must be one and understand each other in whatever we are doing.... She showed ability from an early age. She could make miracles. When she grabbed something, she never let go.... After she won, I was so happy. I felt like flying up to touch the sky. She gave us the kind of status we have now. I remember the village King came to congratulate Caster and said, "my child, you've put me on the map" (Ginnane).

D. Semenya expresses that God made her daughter's body and bestowed her with remarkable athleticism and her family must, and does, accept, understand, and celebrate her the way God made her. In addition, people in their community, including the village King, celebrate C. Semenya's bodily capabilities and what those abilities brought to the community. D. Semenya's testimony tells the viewers that she, as well as the larger community, does not have an issue with C. Semenya's womanhood; rather, outsiders have a problem with her assumed incoherence. Cheryl Cooky et al's study affirms this comment. Western media outlets slandered and questioned C. Semenya, and assumed she was a man, not a real woman, intersex, or a hermaphrodite, whereas almost all South African media outlets defended C. Semenya's female identity and right to bodily autonomy (Cooky et al.).

In an article featured in the *Guardian*, Sekgala also appeals to God: "She [C. Semenya] called me after the heats and told me that they think she's a man. What can I do when they call her a man, when she's really not a man? It is God who made her look that way" (qtd. in "Caster Semenya's Mother"). In addition to the notion that her femininity is innate, as signified by her genitals, Sekgala reminds viewers that her granddaughter was made by God, and, therefore, there is nothing wrong with her apparent masculinity. C. Semenya's masculine characteristics do not negate her femaleness. Although the media assumes the mothers have privileged knowledge about the child they raised and C. Semenya has always identified as a woman, many Western viewers may be compelled (see Cooky et al.) to privilege secular, Western scientific discourses to which the IAAF appeals. These discourses suggest that C. Semenya is not, or must not be, a normal or real woman. They suggest that she is intersex; she has a DSD.

The practice of looking at genitals to determine one's sex and gender is common all over the world in and outside of medical contexts. Looking at one's genitals is believed to reveal or signify one's sex and gender (Karkazis, *Fixing Sex*; Kessler; Butler; Fausto-Sterling, *Sexing the Body*). D. Semenya and Sekgala both rely on this logic when questioned. However, scientific discourses claim that sex is more complicated than the appearance of one's external genitalia. According to these discourses, one's external genitalia, internal reproductive system, gonadal tissue, chromosomes, and hormone levels together determine one's sex as male or female. If one's body "flutters ... between sexes"

(Karkazis, *Fixing Sex* 95)—for example, if a woman's testosterone levels are "too" high, if one's chromosomes do not "match" one's external genitalia, or if one has variant genitals—one is ostensibly incoherent, disordered, and assumed to be unfairly advantaged in the realm of sport. This narrative, however, is still invested in the cissexist and interphobic notion that to be a real woman, one must have certain bodily attributes.

Featured in the documentary speaking about C. Semenya, Nick Davies, IAAF spokesperson, reproduces this medical(izing) rhetoric: "It's [Semenya's embodiment] seen as a medical condition. That's a point to stress" (Ginnane). Emphasizing that C. Semenya's anatomy is a pathological condition functions to remove (maternal) testimonial power and legitimacy from D. Semenya and Sekgala as well as from C. Semenya herself. Davies's comment reflects the longstanding practice of delegitimizing mothers' knowledge in the face of medical expertise, which we elaborate in the next section (Apple; Hays; Watson; Wolf). For now, employing medical(izing) rhetoric enables the IAAF to, in Georgiann Davis's words, "reclaim their authority and jurisdiction" (57) over C. Semenya's apparently intersex body.[5] Emphasizing that her body is disordered also reproduces the sex and gender binary.

Both the medical discourse and investment in sex and gender binaries, despite their incoherence, are evident in the IAAF's policies about testosterone levels. According to the IAAF, normal men have levels above 10.5 nmol/L and normal women have levels ranging from 0.1 to 2.8 nmol/L (Zeigler). Given these ranges, trans women athletes who want to compete are required to maintain testosterone levels below 10 nmol/L by taking hormones to disrupt their natural hormone levels for at least twelve months prior to competition. Although the regulations demanding women with the intersex variation hyper-androgenism undergo hormone replacement therapy were suspended in 2015 because of the Court of Arbitration for Sport case between athlete Dutee Chand and the IAAF, the regulations may be reinstated soon (Brown; Karkazis, "One-Track Minds"; Kelner and Rudd; "Semenya"; Agence France-Presse; Beswick). Recall that it does not necessarily follow that people who naturally fall outside of these levels, which are only statistically average, fail their sex or gender or are inherently abnormal, disordered, or unfairly advantaged. As mentioned earlier, neither testosterone nor sex characteristics are the irreducible root of one's athletic abilities (Dworkin and Cooky; Zaccone; Jordan-Young and Karkazis; Karkazis, "The Ignorance"; Simpson et al. 2000).

The most violent outcome of this pathologizing narrative is unnecessary and irreversible medical intervention, including hormone therapy and intersex genital mutilation (IGM) (Chase; Karkazis, *Fixing Sex*; Jordon-Young; M. Holmes; M. Holmes, ed.; Guillot et al.). Davis elaborates on the assumed need to quickly re-order "unruly" (Fausto-Sterling, *Sexing the Body* 8) intersex infants and children via unnecessary and irreversible medical interventions:

> Medical professionals who frame intersex as an emergency are creating a state of exception that allows them to abandon medical ethics that warn against performing medically unnecessary surgery on children. Once the intersex trait is presented as an emergency and the state of exception is established, medical providers tend to inundate parents with information about intersex. However, the information they present focuses on the alignment of sex, gender, and sexuality as essentialist characteristics of the body, laying the groundwork for justifying medically unnecessary inter-ventions notably irreversible surgical procedures that many doctors continue to, even today, recommend without any hesitation to parents of newly diagnosed children. (23)

Davis brilliantly points out how medical professionals abandon medical ethics by establishing a state of exception (Pagonis). In line with Davis's reasoning, we maintain that with the aid of sensationalist and misrepresentative Western media, IAAF policies (e.g., retaining the right to sex test suspect athletes and preventing athletes from competing) establish a similar state of exception and, in turn, institute discriminatory, humiliating, and invasive policies that are not in line with medical ethics. In contrast, Sekgala and D. Semenya's accounts work to resist this sense of emergency and exception. Even though these women's views about biology, sex, and gender are debatable and debatably discriminatory, they serve the important purpose of combating this frenzied state of exception that not only led to C. Semenya's discriminatory exclusion but also could lead, or could have led, to coercive, irreversible, and/or mutilating bodily interventions.

When a state of exception is established, as was the case with C. Semenya, the state must be resolved; the person's so-called true sex must be revealed and reordered. The IAAF and IOC enforced this reordering of women athletes' bodies by mandating normalization surgeries on women's sexual anatomy. Rebecca Jordan-Young et al. report that several women athletes were forced to undergo medically unnecessary partial clitorectomies and/or gonadectomies to become properly competition—ready—to become properly sexed women. The mandate for irrevocable and medically unnecessary surgeries for both trans women athletes and women athletes with intersex traits has been abolished (Zeiger; Tourjee). However, as noted above, depending on the verdict of Chand and the IAAF case, women athletes may be forced to undergo hormone replacement therapy. Supported by authoritative, yet interphobic and cissexist ideologies, medical and scientific recommendations to irreversibly alter women's bodies draw from the same ideological foundation that D. Semenya and Sekgala also draw from: one must have certain biological traits to be a real woman. Such policies do not apply and have never applied to male athletes.

Although this medico-scientific discourse helpfully rejects that sex is readily visible, it reproduces the sex binary and the notion that one's fundamental sex and gender can be determined by medical investigation. Contrary to D. Semenya and Sekgala's commonsense discourse and the dominant medico-scientific dichotomous understanding of sex, feminist, intersex, and queer studies scholars as well as feminist science studies researchers "view the body not as essence, but as a bare scaffolding on which discourses and performance build a completely accultured being" (Fausto-Sterling, *Sexing the Body* 6). Sex "is not a pure physical category;" "scientists create truth about sexuality," biology, sex, and gender (Fausto-Sterling 2000, *Sexing the Body*, 4, 5). Sex is not discovered by investigation. Sex is (re)created in, through, and by culture. Hence, the sex binary is not a natural or objective fact. Sex, like gender, is a social construct; ideas about gender precede sex (Davis; Dreger, ed.; Herdt; Potter; Hird; Jordan-Young; Kessler; M. Holmes, ed.; M. Holmes; Fausto-Sterling; Karkazis, *Fixing Sex*; Laqueur; Daston and Galison; Haraway; Butler).

Consequently, when one looks at C. Semenya's body to evaluate, for example, her speed, androgen levels, genital formation, chromosomes, gender performance, and secondary sex characteristics, what one sees or does not see is informed by hegemonic standards of femininity.[6] Some of these standards include low testosterone levels, a vagina, a uterus, ovaries, XX chromosomes, visible breasts, unmuscular body, less able or athletic than men, thin, and white (Collins). According to these standards, C. Semenya fails and is read as suspect woman and as suspect intersex.

Maternal Testimony under Colonial Gaze

In light of the above analysis, it may be tempting to disregard D. Semenya's and Sekgala's narratives as scientifically or theoretically inaccurate and discriminatory. However, to do so would neglect the historical context and the colonial, racist construction of African women's bodies at play in this case. As Brenna Munro explains, "the inspection of [C.] Semenya's body seems driven in part ... by a familiar prurient/Enlightenment will-to-know" (391) the objective scientific truth. The inspection seems driven by the assumed (and institutionalized) right to investigate her body. And this "will-to-know" and impulse to pathologize her Black, female, and apparently disordered body has historical roots in colonial, racist scientific projects. Moreover, neglecting to seriously engage with and bear witness to D. Semenya's and Sekgala's testimonies reproduces the historical dismissal of Black women's, colonized peoples', and mothers' narratives of themselves, their experiences, and their families.

There is a long Western, colonial, imperial, and scientific history of labelling African women's genitals, particularly South African women's genitals, ambiguous and primitive which functions, therefore, to construct European bodies as superior for supposedly embodying the sex binary (Magubane; Reis; Gilman, *Difference and Pathology*, "The Hottentot and the Prostitute"; Singer; Daniels). Since the seventeenth century (Magubane, "Spectacles and Scholarship" 769)—sometimes citing Western, European, male colonizers' travelling texts and tales of "discovery" (Flower and Murie; Beck and Beck)—European, American, and South African medical texts maintained that "malformed or ambiguous genitalia ... were particularly common among women of African descent—a 'fixed peculiarity of race'" (Magubane, "Spectacles and Scholarship" 769; and Waitz; Beck and Beck; Flower and Murie; Velpeau; Cuvier; Otto; Müller; Von Luschka et al.). These authors did not deny that European women also can have "*unusual formations of the generative organs"* or "malconformations," but they emphasized, "it is not common in Europe, but is frequent in warmer climates" (emphasis in original, Beck and Beck, 175-76). The malconformations (also known as "Hottentot aprons") these writers ostensibly viewed and inspected were "excessive" in clitoral length and/or labia minora visibility (Somerville 26; McClintock 42; Magubane, "Spectacles and Scholarship" 769). Many writers and scientists claimed that these malconformations were literal markers of innate, perverse, and insatiable sexuality, as well as degeneration and primitivism (Gilman, *Difference and Pathology* 90; Roen 18). As a result, an African woman "becomes her genitalia" (Gilman, *Difference and Pathology* 121); she is reduced to her genital formation.

Some European, American, and South African medico-scientific texts published well into the twentieth century continued to perpetuate the idea that African and Black women were sexually ambiguous (Magubane, "Spectacles and Scholarship"; Charlewood; Ramsay et al.).[7] Western nations as well as South Africa during apartheid were (and still are) invested in biological racism and white supremacy: beliefs underpinned by or intersect with interphobia and impose "intersex citizenship" status (Grabham 29). Sport sex testing is one way by which these discriminatory views and oppressive consequences currently manifest.

One of the most noteworthy historical examples of this violence is the racist and sexist public display and objectification of Sara Saartjie Baartman's supposedly malformed and excessive sexual anatomy (Gordon-Chipembere; Gilman, *Difference and Pathology*, "The Hottentot and the Prostitute"; Munro; McClintock; Singer; Willis; R. Holmes). Baartman was, in Munro's terms, "a travelling human exhibit of racial and sexual difference" (390). Baartman died in Paris in 1815, and her body was dismembered and dissected by Georges Cuvier. Some of her sexual anatomy was pickled and put on display in the *Musee de l'Homme* in Paris and remained on display for public viewing for around 160 years. Her body was not returned to the area of her birth, the Gamtoos River Valley in the Eastern Cape of South Africa, until 2002. With this history of objectifying, pathologizing, displaying, and dissecting Black women's bodies,

[f]or South Africans, the questioning of [C.] Semenya's sex not only brings to mind apartheid's categorizations of people into racial groups—a traumatic and chaotic process that involved the

inspection of people's bodies on a nationwide scale—but calls up the life-story of Sara Baartman, a chapter of imperial history that has been central to post-apartheid nationalist discourse. (Munro 390)

Similarly, Neville Hoad reasons that the details leaked supposedly outlining C. Semenya's biological characteristics "contain immense symbolic violence, evoking images of vivisection and willy-nilly the shameful history of Sarah Baartman, who was literally cut up and turned inside out for the world to see by Cuvier" (401-2). Reminiscent of Baartman's objectification, we witness C. Semenya be reduced to her sex, put on display, and inspected. News headlines like, "Caster Semenya 'is a hermaphrodite', tests show" (Hart) and "Caster Semenya has male sex organs and no womb or ovaries" (Hurst), and the content that scrutinizes her supposed sex traits are just a couple of representations that reduce her to her sex (Cooky et al.). Eerily evoking Baartman, C. Semeya's body is objectified and analyzed piece by piece by "objective" medical professionals seeking the truth.[8]

Taking the complex, colonial history into account draws attention to the way supposed degenerate sexual ambiguity was, and remains, imagined and constructed by colonial and imperial forces across gender, racial, national, and geographical lines. Perceived sexual ambiguity and intersex has been and continues to be used as a colonial and imperial tool to render certain people and nations degenerate and suspect, and to justify various forms of violence. This history contextualizes the violence enacted on C. Semenya; it demonstrates that the violence she endured and continues to endure must be read as a contemporary iteration of the "ambiguously" sexed African woman (Magubane, "Spectacles and Scholarship"; Munro), and it contextualizes her mother and grandmother's support.

D. Semenya's and Sekgala's comments are, thus, not simply dismissible as unscientific or discriminatory. As Hoad writes, too many scholars who talk about C. Semenya "display little awareness of the history of the scientific gaze on the gendered and sexualized black body for, at least, the last three hundred years" (398). This lack of awareness could reckon D. Semenya's and Sekgala's assertions about the apparent visual nature of sex as uneducated, backward, or interphobic. Instead, their assertions must be read against the backdrop of Western colonialism, imperialism, and biological racism.

This lack of historical awareness led some scholars not only to treat intersex "as though it had an ontological status in all times and places" (Magubane, "Spectacles and Scholarship" 767) but also to disparage C. Semenya's defenders' rejection of the label "intersex." Without historical context, these scholars reduce such a rejection to interphobia. In addition to C. Semenya's mother's and grandmother's support and insistence that C. Semenya is "a girl not a boy" (cultural critics Anderson), South African news outlets (Cooky et al.), various politicians, and Leonard Chuene—former president of Athletics South Africa (ASA) who resigned in protest from the IAAF board for "castigat[ing]" C. Semenya (qtd. by Munro 2010: 386)—all voiced support for her. Chuene publically announced, "I'm fuming. This girl has been castigated from day one, based on what? ... There's no scientific evidence. You can't say somebody's child is not a girl. You denounce my child as a boy when she's a girl? If you did that to my child, I'd shoot you" (qtd. in Munro 386; also see Dixon). Chuene is correct that there is no conclusive evidence demonstrating she has an unfair advantage. Moreover, his statement also supports C. Semenya's caregivers' knowledge and recognizes their authority.

Taking a different approach to defending C. Semenya via rejecting intersex, South African politician Julius Malema has stated the following:

Hermaphrodite, what is that? Somebody tell me, what is hermaphrodite in Pedi? There's no such thing, hermaphrodite, in Pedi. So don't impose your hermaphrodite concepts on us.... Why should we be told today our children are hermaphrodites? She's a girl and why should we accept concepts that are imposed on us by the imperialists? We will never agree to that concept. You are either a girl or a boy and that's it. (Malema qtd. in Hoad 400)

With this sort of pejorative statement, many people conflated claiming intersex with modernity and, since it was explicitly rejected by some of C. Semenya's supporters, they were presented as backward and discriminatory (Munro; Magubane, "Spectacles and Scholarship"). But Malema's statements cannot be reduced to interphobia; these words come from an anti-imperial politic. It would be similarly reductionist to dismiss D. Semenya's and Sekgala's statements as discriminatory, and it is instructive to take a more nuanced reading. As Malema's assertions suggest, as well as Brenna Munro and Zine Magubane ("Spectacles and Scholarship") remind, rejecting intersex and defending C. Semenya's womanhood must be read alongside the complex imperial history of South Africa.

Drawing from Munro and Antje Schuhmann, Magubane also describes some feminist scholars' confusion with South Africa's support for C. Semenya: "scholars found it particularly hard to reconcile popular support for Semenya with South Africa's purportedly rampant homophobia and endemic 'homophobic hate crimes' (Schuhmann 95)" (766). Some scholars reconciled this supposed incongruence by "dismissing the support Semenya received as a manifestation of racially essentialist and chauvinistic black nationalism, which, by definition, could not accommodate identities [or bodies] that 'complicate this male/female binary' (Munro 391)" (Magubane, "Spectacles and Scholarship" 767). This logic ignores the historical context of Western colonial forces imposing biological racism. Ultimately, equating the concept of intersex with modernity, liberalism, progress, or feminism and imposing that notion ignores how imperialism and colonialism have constructed sexual ambiguity; it continues the imperial work of imposing bodily categories onto colonized nations and people, especially Black women.

Considering the media's treatment of C. Semenya's caregivers in this nuanced context also gives meaning to the position of maternal testimony in relation to sex and gender. For one, reliance upon their testimony represents a feminist challenge to professional, medical expertise by the privileged knowledge of women—knowledge that has been disregarded, particularly in the realm of caregiving, in recent decades (O'Reilly; Zeitlin and Rowshan). Their testimony could also represent the media's demand for anecdotal evidence when scientific evidence is inconclusive, or worse, not convincing or not supported by commonsense narratives about sex and gender. In other words, in a moment when medico-scientific discourse fails to give sufficient proof—thus failing to reestablish traditional femininity with respect to a sex and gender binary—journalists, citing C. Semenya's caregivers, turn to the myth of the visible nature of sex.

Further complicating the treatment of C. Semenya's caregivers is the fact that drawing on maternal testimony for the privileged information of caregivers echoes the historical bias that women, as carers, have a closer relationship than men to nature. This logic is also racialized to position Black women further from cultural production than white women (Gilman, "Black Bodies"). It has justified women's exclusion from the political arena and access to power, relegating mothers and their expertise to the domestic sphere (Bloch and Bloch; Lister). However, the professionalization and colonial expansion of Western medicine over the past century has seen mothers' knowledge about their children regularly overridden by medical experts (Apple; Nathoo and Ostry; Wolf). Even as biomedical literature is constantly updated and expert prescriptions change, the doctor-expert continues to be positioned as more knowledgeable than the mother, particularly when it comes to the domain of pediatrics.[9]

As demonstrated, reducing C. Semenya's mothers' (and nation's) support to an interphobic backlash or merely an attempt to protect C. Semenya neglects the historical context of colonization and ongoing biological racism that hurts Black women, particularly in sport, as sex-testing practices demonstrate (Magubane, "Spectacles and Scholarship"; Entine; Hoberman; Harrison and Lawrence; Miller; Charlewood; Ramsay et al.). We argue that D. Semenya and Sekgala's comments about C. Semenya's body and womanhood must also be read as opposing imperial forces seeking to name and define South African women's bodies. Undermining and subsequently ignoring their comments because they are apparently interphobic, backward, or antiscience reproduces colonial violence and the historical dismissal of Black, colonized, maternal, and women's narratives. Moreover, we argue overlooking D. Semenya's and Sekgala's testimony neglects the fact that they expand the strict confines of femininity and challenge the dominant ethos that authentic femininity is frail, unmuscular, less able or athletic than men, and white.

Femininity Is Not Contradictory to Athleticism

In addition to the idea that one's sexual anatomy and gender identity must coincide (Butler; Fausto-Sterling, *Sexing the Body*; Karkazis, *Fixing Sex*), one's gender performance and abilities must match. For instance, women are assumed to be naturally less athletically inclined or capable because of their apparently naturally smaller, daintier, less muscular bodies. Further, as mentioned above, authentic or idealized femininity is white (Collins 2004). As Vikki Krane explains, "the underlying message is that athleticism and femininity are contradictory" (115; also see Dworkin and Cooky; Cahn; Cohen; McDonagh and Pappano). Although we see, for example, differences in elite women's and men's running times (Vilain), these differences "can be attributed to social, political, economic, and psychological discrimination rather than biological factors" (Travers 90; also see Adams and Leavitt; Chadwick et al.; Cunningham; Cahn; Kanagy and Kraybill; Billings and Young; Daddario; Hall; Fink; Kane). One clear example of this systemic sexist discrimination is the institutionalization of sex testing women athletes because they appear too masculine or are too athletically inclined.[10]

C. Semenya's mothers, however, do not seem perturbed by the fact that C. Semenya does not cohere according to dominant standards of femininity. "It [the sex testing controversy] never went to my head," Sekgala explains, because C. Semenya is "a girl" (Ginnane). Likewise, "when they started saying she's not a girl, she's a boy, I never had a problem," D. Semenya clarifies, because "she's a girl not a boy" (Ginnane). They actively accept C. Semenya's masculine physique, celebrate her capabilities and feminine identity, and remain resolute that she is an authentic woman. "She showed ability from an early age," D. Semenya states proudly, "she could make miracles" (Ginnane). C. Semenya's mothers reject the idea that womanhood and femininity are contradictory with athleticism, muscularity, and stereotypically unfeminine gender performances. In doing so, they challenge dominant Western ideas of femininity. Bearing witness to D. Semenya and Sekgala's testimonies that do not regard C. Semenya's body, gender identity, and abilities as incongruous, viewers are provided with the opportunity to reexamine dominant ideologies about femininity, masculinity, and pathology.

Regardless of Being Cleared "Officially" ...

Even though C. Semenya was cleared to compete again about a year after the initial speculation, questions of her sex, body, and gender remained in the news when she won silver at the London 2012 Olympic Games, when she married her longtime girlfriend, Violet Raseboya, in 2015, and as she was on track to compete in the Rio de Janeiro 2016 Olympics. "Even now," Karkazis states, "six years on, as she prepares for Rio, nearly every report on Semenya's race times doggedly refers to this [sex-test] investigation" ("One-Track Minds"). After she won gold for the 800m in Rio, the media and her fellow competitors continued to question, slander, and delegitimize her achievement by claiming she was unfairly advantaged due to her supposed intersex or male biology (Karkazis, "The Ignorance"). Consider, for example, *The Telegraph's* story "Caster Semenya Destroys Rest of the Field to Claim *Easy* Gold in Women's 800m Final—Can Anyone Beat Her?" (our emphasis, Bloom). The author, Ben Bloom, claims C. Semenya won with "minimum effort." Demonstrating that, yes, other athletes have beaten C. Semenya, Bloom presumptuously rationalizes the fact that she did not break a world record because "she prioritised gold over records." Smacking of racism and white entitlement, her fellow competitor, Poland's Joanna Jóźwik, remarked after finishing fifth in the event, "I'm glad I'm the first European, the second white" to cross the line (qtd. in Karkazis, "The Ignorance"). C. Semenya's incredible achievements, training, sacrifices, and dedication to the sport are effectively erased and delegitimized (Karkazis, "The Ignorance").

And C. Semenya is in the news again (Kelner and Rudd; "Semenya"; Agence France-Presse; Beswick) because of a recently published, methodologically dubious study (Bermon and Garnier).[11] The authors claim women athletes with high levels of testosterone have an unfair advantage. Of the forty-three athletic events tested in the study, there were apparently five events in which women with higher levels of testosterone had a statically significant advantage. This study will be used as evidence in the case between Chand and the IAAF to support forcing women athletes with testosterone levels that are too high to take hormone replacement therapy. News articles citing C. Semenya not only represent this study as definitive fact, they also postulate that Semenya may end up being forced to level her supposed unfair advantage by taking hormones. However, the study is methodologically unsound and, therefore, the findings are invalid. Gid M-K elaborates, in running their statistical analyses, the authors neglect to perform an

"adjustment for multiple comparisons" to check whether the significance is real or more likely just an artifact of chance ... there is a good chance that this [the results] was just down to luck. So I went through the paper and ran ... a Bonferroni Correction. What this basically does is raise the bar for statistical significance according to the number of tests that had been done. According to these results, none of them are actually significant....

[In the study] you'll notice that there are 16 insignificant results many of which had women with low levels beating women with high levels. From these results we could just as easily conclude that, for the majority of athletic events, testosterone levels had no impact on performance whatsoever. (emphasis in original)

This questionable study is ratcheting up what it takes to be a woman athlete and may have profoundly harmful consequences for women athletes, particularly women athletes of colour and women athletes with (suspect) intersex traits.

Although D. Semenya and Sekgala do not explicitly challenge hegemonic standards of femininity, Len Anderson unequivocally points to these harmful ideologies in the *Sowetan*, one of the largest South African newspapers: "It is very clear that the IAAF used Western stereotypes of what a woman should look like as probable cause [for sex testing C. Semenya] and that is racist and sexist." He continues, "those making the determination [about sex testing] are fat and ugly European men."

Still, it is undeniable that D. Semenya and Sekgala's understandings of sex and gender rely on discriminatory ideologies about the visual and dichotomous nature of sex and gender. Indeed, there are other ways to protect C. Semenya from symbolic and literal violence and celebrate her femininity and identity other than reinforcing the sex and gender binary (Hoad 402). Nevertheless, ignoring their resistance is to decontextualize their accounts as Black South African women in a colonial relationship to Western media, culture, and science.

Magubane notes that "we may find statements like [Malema's] 'don't impose your hermaphrodite concepts on us' to be inelegant" ("Spectacles and Scholarship" 768) or interphobic. Likewise, we may find D. Semenya's and Sekgala's statements scientifically incorrect, antithetical to science, or interphobic. These sorts of assertions, though, provide feminist scholars with the opportunity to "consider the roles race and imperial history have played in constituting intersex" (Magubane, "Spectacles and Scholarship" 768), sexual "ambiguity," and DSD. Moreover, D. Semenya's and Sekgala's maternal testimonies provide motherhood scholars with the opportunity to consider how maternal testimony can both reproduce and challenge dominant ideas about caregivers and expertise—and testimonies must be situated intersectionally for their meaning to be fully appreciated.

Endnotes

1   Speaking of her grandmother, C. Semenya states, "she's the most important person in my life because she was the head of this house. So, when our parents aren't around she's the one taking care of us. She's my parent actually" (Ginnane).

2   Cary Gabriel Costello has coined the term "interphobia" to describe the systemic violent discrimination against intersex people, people with intersex traits, and people thought to have intersex traits. Interphobia is another term for intersexphobia (Viloria). It is evidenced by, for example, the common practice of intersex genital mutilation (IGM); employing reproductive technologies to ensure infants with intersex anatomy are not born; and invasive medical exams and media treatment of such athletes as C. Semenya (Cooky Dycus, and Dworkin; Magubane; Chase; Davis; Karkazis, *Fixing Sex*; Kessler; Fausto-Sterling; Orr).

3   Santhi Soundarajan (1981-) (India), and Pinki Pramanik (1986-) (India), Margaret Wambui (1995-) (Kenya), Francine Niyonsaba (1993-) (Burundi), and Dutee Chand (1996-) (India) have either been subjected to sex testing or have been publically questioned about their sex. Soundarajan was tested in 2006; Chand was tested in 2014; and Pramanik's sex accusations and testing arose in 2012 after she was accused of raping a woman she lived with (Mitra, "Male/Female or Other). Questions of Wambui's and Niyonsaba's sex and accusations that they are men, intersex, or hermaphrodites float around public media forums (Gugal; Harper). These accusations have increased since Wambui won bronze and Niyonsaba won silver for the 800m race at the 2016 Rio de Janeiro Olympics. Moreover, although many scholars and journalists assume and impose DSD and intersex (as diagnosis and identity) on these women, none of these athletes have publicly claimed DSD or intersex.

4   In other words, drawing from Judith Butler, D. Semenya's and Sekgala's account tell us that C. Semenya's entrance into the social world was not halted by an inability to be immediately sexed and, by extension, gendered.

5   The medical community adopted DSD terminology in favour of "intersex" about a decade ago. Davis argues in *Contesting Intersex*

that this shift enabled medical professionals to reclaim their jurisdiction over people with intersex variations: "the renaming of *intersex* as *disorders of sex development* allowed medical professionals to reclaim their authority and jurisdiction over intersex, which had come under fire from intersex activism, feminist critiques of intersex medicalization, and [John] Money's exposure" (emphasis in original, 57). DSD language is employed by the IAAF, as Davies's medicalizing comment illustrates.

6   In Suzanne Kessler's terms, "How hard one 'looks' at genitals and what one 'sees' [i.e. ambiguity, ab/normality] is not constrained by the optic nerve but by ideology" (44-45). Or, in Sara Ahmed's terms, what we perceive depends on how we are orientated.

7   In *Bantu Gynaecology*, Godfrey P. Charlewood asserts that intersex congenital "abnormalities" are more frequent in "Negroes and related races" (12). Michele Ramsay and colleagues similarly claim that there is a "high frequency" of "true hermaphroditism" and external genital "ambiguity" "among southern African blacks" (4): "In southern Africa, ambiguous genitalia seems to be much more common in blacks than in whites" (9).

8   When we speak of race and African and Black people we are not conflating Blackness with African identity or citizenship and we are not merely retrospectively applying contemporary understandings of Black, white, race, or racism onto historical contexts. Race, whiteness, and Blackness have been constructed very differently through time and space (Magubane, "Which Bodies Matter?"; Schiebinger; McClintock; Goldberg; Stoler; Willis). Race categories were, and in many respects remain, unsteady. When we speak of the historical construction of many African women's bodies and genitals, we do not suggest they understood themselves to be or thought themselves Black or that they were necessarily understood to be Black by others. Nevertheless, the shift in racial/racist discourses and beliefs that rooted Blackness in, for example darker skin and hair texture, occurred alongside the maintenance of the belief in sexually ambiguous African women and African women were constructed as Black. That is, our aim here is to trace the ideological construction and imposition of sexual ambiguity to contextualize how this construction and imposition is articulated through current sex testing practices.

9   The case of infant feeding is a one clear example of this effect: from prescribing and supervising the distribution of formula in the 1950s to exclusively promoting breastfeeding in contemporary hospitals, mothers are expected to follow the scientifically-determined order of the day as it changes (Nathoo and Ostry).

10 Another clear example of this sexist discrimination is the reason why sex segregation in sport came into being. Cooky and Dworkin explain that sex segregation in sport was "put forward historically when women outperformed men at athletic performances" (22). Sport sex segregation was not instituted to reflect innate gendered or sexed capacities but rather to preserve "images of male superiority" (McDonagh and Pappano 17). Ideologies about women's assumed inferior athletic abilities have led to decades of literal and symbolic violence against women athletes that have material consequences on women's performances.

11 The study was funded by the IAAF and one of the authors, Stéphane Bermon, works for the IAAF.

Works Cited

Adams, Carly, and Stacey Leavitt. "'It's Just Girls' Hockey': Troubling Progress Narratives in Girls' and Women's Sport." *International Review for the Sociology of Sport*, 2016, pp. 1-21.

Agence France-Presse "Testosterone a 'Significant' Boost for Women Athletes." *New Visions: Uganda's Leading Daily*, 4 July 2017, www.newvision.co.ug/new_vision/news/1456881/testosterone-significant-boost-women-athletes. Accessed 7 July 2017.

Ahmed, Sara. *Queer Phenomenology*. Duke University Press, 2006.

Amy-Chinn, Dee. "Doing Epistemic (In)justice to Semenya." *International Journal of Media and Cultural Politics,* vol. 6, no. 3, 2011, pp. 311-26.

Anderson, Len. "On What Basis Was Caster Tested?" *The Sowetan*, 24 Aug. 2009, www.sowetanlive.co.za/sowetan/archive/2009/08/24/on-what-basis-was -caster-tested. Accessed 20 Jan. 2016.

Apple, Rima. *Perfect Motherhood: Science and childrearing in America*. Rutgers University Press, 2006.

Beck, Theodric Romeyn, and John B. Beck. "Chapter IV. Doubtful Sex." *Elements of Medical Jurisprudence, vol. 1*, Lippincott, 1860, pp. 164-187.

Beck, Theodric Romeyn, and John B. Beck. *Evidence of Medical Jurisprudence Vol. 1*. Lippincott, 1863.

Bermon, Stéphane, and Pierre-Yves Garmier. "Serum Androgen Levels and Their Relation to Performance in Track and Field: Mass Spectrometry Results from 2127 Observations in Male and Female Elite Athletes." *British Journal of Sports Medicine*, 2017, pp. 1-7.

Beswick, Emma. "Caster Semenya may have to take medication as study reopens testosterone debate." *Euronews*, 4 July 2017, www.euronews.com/2017/07/04/caster-semenya-may-have-to-take-testosterone-medication-as-study-reopens-debate. Accessed 7 July 2017.

Billings, Andrew, and Brittany D. Young. "Comparing Flagship News Programs: Women's Sport Coverage in ESPN's *SportsCenter* and FOX Sports 1's *Fox Sports Live*." *Electronic News*, vol. 9, no. 1, 2015, pp. 3-16.

Bloch, Maurice, and Jean H. Bloch. "Women and the Dialectics of Nature in Eighteenth Century French Thought." *Nature, Culture and Gender*, edited by Carol P. MacCormack and Marilyn Strathern, Cambridge University Press, 1980, pp. 25-41.

Bloom, Ben. "Caster Semenya Destroys Rest of the Field to Claim *Easy* Gold in Women's 800m Final—Can Anyone Beat Her?" *The Telegraph*, 21 Aug. 2016, www.telegraph.co.uk/olympics/2016/08/20/caster-semenya-womens-800m-final-rio-olympics-lynsey-sharp-team/. Accessed 25 Aug. 2016.

Brady, Anita. "'Could This Women's World Champ Be a Man?': Caster Semenya and the Limits of Being Human." *AntePodium*, 2011, pp 1-16.

Brown, Andy. "CAS Suspend IAAF's Hyperandrogenism Regulations." *Sports Integrity Initiative*, 27 July 2015, www.sportsintegrityinitiative.com/cas-suspends-iaafs-hyperandrogenism-regulations/. Accessed 9 July 2017.

Brown, Andy. "IAAF Study Shows Chand Case Is Far from Over." *Sports Integrity Initiative*, 5 July 2017, www.sportsintegrityinitiative.com/iaaf-study-shows-chand-case-far/. Accessed 9 July 2017.

Butler, Judith. *Gender Trouble*. 1990. Routledge, 2006.

Butler, Judith. "Performative Acts and Gender Constitution: An Essay in Phenomenology and Feminist Theory." *Theatre Journal*, vol. 40, no. 4, 1988, pp. 519-31.

Butler, Judith. *Undoing Gender*. Routledge, 2004.

Buzuvis, Erin E. "Caster Semenya and the Myth of the Level Playing Field." *The Modern America*, vol. 6, no. 2, 2010, pp. 36-42.

Camporesi, Silvia, and Paolo Maugeri. "Unfair Advantage and the Myth of the Level Playing Field in IAAF and IOC Policies on Hyperandrogenism: When Is It Fair to Be a Woman?" *Gender Testing in Sport: Ethics, Cases and Controversies*, edited by Sandy Montañoia and Aurélie Olivesi, Routledge, 2016, pp. 46-59.

"Caster Semenya's Mother Hits Out at Gender Dispute." *The Guardian*, 20 Aug. 2009, www.theguardian.com/sport/2009/aug/20/caster-semenya-gender-world-championship-dispute. Accessed 7 Mar. 2016.

Cavanagh, Sheila L., and Heather Sykes. "Transsexual Bodies at the Olympics: The International Olympic Committee's Policy on Transsexual Athletes at the 2004 Athens Summer Games." *Body and Society*, vol. 12, no. 3, 2006, pp. 75-102.

Chadwick, Simon, et al., editors. *Routledge Handbook of Sports Marketing*. Routledge, 2016.

De la Chapelle, Albert. "The Use and Misuse of Sex Chromatin Screening for 'Gender Identification' of Female Athletes." *The Journal of the American Medical Association*, vol. 256, no. 4, 1986, pp. 1920-23.

Charlewood, Godfrey P. *Bantu Gynaecology*. University of Witwatersrand Press, 1956.

Chase, Cheryl. "Hermaphrodites with Attitude: Mapping the Emergence of Intersex Political Activism." *GLQ*, vol. 4, no. 2, 1998, pp. 189-211.

Chase, Cheryl. "Hermaphrodites with Attitude: Mapping the Emergence of Intersex Political Activism." *The Transgender Studies Reader*, edited by Susan Stryker and Stephan Whittle, Routledge, 2006, pp. 300-14.

Cohen, Marilyn. *No Girls in the Clubhouse: The Exclusion of Women from Baseball*. McFarland Press, 2009.

Collins, Patricia Hill. *Black Sexual Politics: African Americans, Gender and the New Racism*. Routledge, 2004.

Cooky, Cheryl, and Shari L. Dworkin. "Policing the Boundaries of Sex: A Critical Examination of Gender Verification and the Caster Semenya Controversy." *Journal of Sex Research*, vol. 50, no. 2, 2013, pp 103-11.

Cooky, Cheryl, et al. "'What Makes a Woman a Woman?' Versus 'Our First Lady of Sport': A Comparative Analysis of the United States and the South African Media Coverage of Caster Semenya." *Journal of Sport and Social Issues*, vol. 37, no. 1, 2013, pp 31-56.

Cooper, Emily J. "Gender Testing in Athletic Competitions—Human Rights Violations: Why Michael Phelps Is Praised and Caster Semenya Is Chastised." *The Journal of Gender, Race, and Justice*, vol. 14, no. 1, 2010, pp 233-64.

Costello, Cary Gabriel. "Interphobia—Not Cured by Hiding Us Away." *The Intersex Roadshow*, 12 Sept. 2010, intersexroadshow. blogspot.ca/2010/09/interphobia-not-cured-by-hiding-us-away.html. Accessed 17 July 2015.

Cunningham, George B. "Media Coverage of Women's Sport: A New Look at an Old Problem."*Physical Educator*, vol. 60, no. 2, 2003, pp. 43-47.

Cuvier, Georges. "Extrait d'observations faite sur le cadavre d'une femme connue à Paris et à Londres sous le nom de Vénus Hottentotte." *Memoires du Musée d'histoire naturelle*, vol. 3, 1817, pp. 259-274.

Daddario, Gina. *Women's Sport and Spectacle: Gendered Television Coverage and the Olympic Games*. Praeger, 1998.

Daniels, Yolande J. "Exhibit A: Private Life without a Narrative." *Black Venus 2010: They Called Her 'Hottentot,'* edited by Deborah Willis, Temple University Press, 2010, pp. 62-67.

Daston, Lorraine, and Peter Galison. *Objectivity*. Zone Books, 2007.

Davis, Georgiann. *Contesting Intersex: The Dubious Diagnosis*. New York University Press, 2015.

Davis, Georgiann. "The Power to Name: Diagnostic Terminology and Diverse Experiences." *Psychology and Sexuality*, vol. 5, no. 1, 2014, pp. 15-27.

Deliovsky, Katerina. *White Femininity: Race, Gender & Power*. Fernwood Publishing, 2010.

Dixon, Robyn. "Runner Caster Semenya has Heard the gender comments all her life." *Los Angeles Times*, 21 Aug. 2009, articles.latimes. com/2009/aug/21/world/fg-south-africa-runner21. Accessed 18 Oct. 2014.

Dreger, Alice Domurat, editor. *Intersex in the Age of Ethics*. University Publishing Group, 1999.

Dworkin, Shari L., and Cheryl Cooky. "Sport, Sex Segregation, and Sex Testing: Critical Reflections on This Unjust Marriage." *The American Journal of Bioethics*, vol. 12, no. 7, 2012, pp. 21-23.

Entine, Jon. *Taboo: Why Black Athletes Dominate Sports and Why We're Afraid to Talk About it*. Public Affairs, 2000.

Fausto-Sterling, Anne. "The Five Sexes, Revisited." *The Sciences*, vol. 40, no. 4, 2000, pp. 18-23.

Fausto-Sterling, Anne. *Sexing the Body*. Basic Books, 2000.

Fink, Janet S. "Female Athletes, Women's Sport, and the Sport Media Commercial Complex: Have We Really 'Come a Long Way, Baby'?" *Sport Management Review*, vol. 18, no. 3, 2015, pp. 331-42.

Flower, W. H., and James Murie. "Account of the Dissection of a Bushwoman." *Journal of Anatomy and Physiology*, vol. 1, 1867, pp. 189-208.

Gilman, Sander. "Black Bodies, White Bodies: Toward an Iconography of Female Sexuality in Late Nineteenth-Century Art, Medicine, and Literature." *Critical Inquiry*, vol. 12, no. 1, 1985, pp. 204-42.

Gilman, Sander. *Difference and Pathology: Stereotypes of Sexuality, Race, and Madness*. Cornell University Press, 1985.

Gilman, Sander. "The Hottentot and the Prostitute: Toward an Iconography of Female Sexuality." *Black Venus 2010: They Called Her 'Hottentot,'* edited by Deborah Willis, Temple University Press, 2010, pp 15-31.

Ginnane, Maxx, director. *Too Fast to be a Woman? The Story of Caster Semenya*. Rise Films/BBC, broadcast BBC2, 22 Feb. 2011.

Goldberg, David Theo, editor. *Anatomy of Racism*. University of Minnesota Press, 1990.

Gordon-Chipembere, Natasha, editor. *Representation and Black Womanhood*. Palgrave Macmillan, 2011.

Grabham, Emily. "Citizen Bodies, Intersex Citizenship." *Sexualities*, vol. 10, no. 29, 2007, pp. 29-48.

Guillot, Vincent, et al. NGO Report to the 7th Periodic Report of France on the Convention against Torture. *Intersex Genital Mutilations: Human Rights Violations Of Persons With Variations Of Sex Anatomy*, 28 Mar. 2016, intersex.shadowreport.org/public/2016-CAT-France-NGO-Zwischen-geschlecht-Intersex-IGM.pdf. Accessed 2 Mar. 2017.

Hall, M. Ann. *The Girl and the Game: A History of Women's Sport in Canada*. University of Toronto Press, 2016.

Hargreaves, Jennifer. *Sporting Females: Critical Issues in the History and Sociology of Women's Sports*. Routledge, 1994.

Haraway, Donna. Simians, Cyborgs, and Women: The Reinvention of Nature. Routledge, 1991.

Haraway, Donna. "Women's Sport, Development, and Cultural Diversity: The South African Experience." *Women's Studies International*, vol. 20, no. 2, 1997, pp. 191-209.

Harper, Joanna. "A Brief History of Intersex Athletes in Sport." *LetsRun*, 19 Sept. 2014, www.letsrun.com/news/2014/09/brief-history-intersex-athletes-sport/?utm_content=bufferce2a6&utm_medium =social&utm_source= facebook.com&utm_campaign=buffer. Accessed 13 Apr. 2016.

Harrison, Keith C., and Suzanne Malia Lawrence. "College Students' Perceptions, Myths, and Stereotypes about African American Athleticism: A Qualitative Investigation." *Sport, Education and Society*, vol. 9, no. 1, 2004, pp. 33-52.

Hart, Simon. "Caster Semenya 'is a hermaphrodite', tests show." *The Telegraph*, 11 Sept. 2009, www.telegraph.co.uk/sport/othersports/ athletics/6170229/Caster-Semenya-is-a-hermaphrodite-tests-show. html. Accessed 9 Jun. 2016.

Hays, Sharon. *The Cultural Contradictions of Motherhood.* Yale University Press, 1996.

Herdt, Gilbert. *Third Sex, Third Gender.* Zone Books, 1994.

Hird, Myra J. "Gender's Nature: Intersexuality, Transsexualism and 'Sex'/'Gender' Binary." *Feminist Theory*, vol. 1, no. 3, 2000, pp. 347-64.

Hoad, Neville. "'Run, Caster Semenya, Run!' Nativism and the Translations of Gender Variance." *Safundi*, vol. 11, no. 4, 2010, pp. 397-405.

Hoberman, John. *Darwin's Athletes: How Sport has Damaged Black America and Preserved the Myth of Race.* Houghton Mifflin Co., 1997.

Holmes, Morgan, editor. *Critical Intersex.* Ashgate Publishing Limited, 2009.

Holmes, Morgan. *Intersex: A Perilous Difference.* Susquehanna University Press, 2008.

Holmes, Morgan. "Introduction: Straddling Past, Present and Future." *Critical Intersex*, edited by Morgan Holmes, Ashgate Publishing Limited, 2009, pp. 1-14.

Holmes, Rachel. *African Queen: The Real Life of the Hottentot Venus.* Random House, 2007.

Holmes, Rachel. *The Hottentot Venus.* Bloomsbury Publishing, 2008.

Hurst, Mike. "Caster Semenya Has Male Sex Organs and No Womb or Ovaries." *The Daily Telegraph*, 11 Sept. 2009, www.dailytelegraph. com.au/sport/semenya-has-no-womb-or-ovaries/story-e6frexni -1225771672245. Accessed 9 Jun. 2016.

Jamieson, Alastair. "Caster Semenya Gender Row: What Is a Hermaphrodite?" *The Telegraph*, 20 Aug. 2009, www.telegraph.co.uk/news/health/news/6060027/Caster-Semenya-gender-row-what-is-a-hermaphrodite.html. Accessed 1 Jun. 2016.

Jordan-Young, Rebecca. *Brain Storm: The Flaws in the Science of Sex Differences*. Harvard University Press, 2010.

Jordan-Young, Rebecca, and Katrina Karkazis. "You Say You're a Woman? That Should Be Enough." *The New York Times*, 17 Jun. 2012, www.nytimes.com/2012/06/18/sports/olympics/olympic-sex-verification-you-say-youre-a-woman-that-should-be-enough.html. Accessed 12 Aug. 2016.

Jordan-Young, Rebecca, et al. "Sex, Health, and Athletes," *British Medical Journal*, vol. 348, 2014, pp. 1-3.

Kanagy, Conrad L., and Donald B. Kraybill. *The Riddles of Human Society*. Pine Forge Press, 1999.

Kane, Mary Jo. "Resistance/Transformation of the Oppositional Binary: Exposing Sport as a Continuum." *Journal of Sport and Social Issues*, vol. 19, no. 2, 1995, pp. 191-218.

Karkazis, Katrina. *Fixing Sex: Intersex, Medical Authority, and Lived Experience*. Duke University Press, 2008.

Karkazis, Katrina. "One-Track Minds: Semenya, Chand & the Violence of Public Scrutiny." *Katrina Karkazis*, 19 July 2016, medium.com/@Karkazis/medias-one-track-mind-semenya-chand-the-violence-of-public-scrutiny-1aa6d1a08454#.q36uqmxqv. Accessed 10 Aug. 2016.

Karkazis, Katrina. "The Ignorance Aimed at Caster Semenya Flies in the Face of the Olympic Spirit." *The Guardian*, 23 Aug. 2016, www.theguardian.com/commentisfree/2016/aug/23/caster-semenya-olympic-spirit-iaaf-athletes-women. Accessed 26 Aug. 2016.

Karkazis, Katrina, and Rebecca Jordan-Young. "The Trouble With Too Much T." *The New York Times*, 10 Apr. 2014, www.nytimes.com/2014/04/11/opinion/the-trouble-with-too-much-t.html?ref=opinion&_r=0. Accessed 9 July 2017.

Kelly, Liz, and Jill Radford. "'Nothing Really Happened': The Invalidation of Women's Experiences of Sexual Violence." *Women, Violence and Male Power: Feminist Activism, Research and Practice*, edited by Marianne Hester et al., Open University Press, 1996, pp. 19-33.

Kelner, Martha, and James Rudd. "Caster Semenya could be forced to undertake hormone therapy for future Olympics." *The Guardian*, 3 July 2017, www.theguardian.com/sport/2017/jul/03/caster-semenya-could-be-forced-to-undertake-hormone-therapy-for-future-olympics. Accessed 4 July 2017.

Kessler, Suzanne J. *Lessons from the Intersex*. Rutgers University Press, 1998.

Kilbourne, Jean. *Killing Us Softly 4: Advertising's Image of Women*. Media Education Foundation, 2010.

Krane, Vikki. "We Can Be Athletic and Feminine, But Do We Want To? Challenging Hegemonic Femininity in Women's Sport." *Quest*, vol. 53, no. 1, 2001, pp. 115-33.

Krane, Vikki, et al. "Living the paradox: Female athletes negotiate femininity and muscularity." *Sex Roles*, vol. 50, no. 5-6, 2004, pp 315-29.

Laqueur, Thomas. *Making Sex: Body and Gender from the Greeks to Freud*. Harvard University Press, 1992.

Levy, Ariel. "Either/Or: Sports, Sex, and the Case of Caster Semenya." *The New Yorker*, 30 Nov. 2009, www.newyorker.com/magazine/2009/11/30/eitheror. Accessed 27 May 2014.

Lister, Ruth. *Feminist Perspectives on Citizenship*. 2nd ed., New York University Press, 2003.

Von Luschka, Hubert, et al. "Die äusseren geschlechtstheile eines Buschweibes." *Monatsschrift für Geburtskunde*, vol. 32, 1868, pp. 343-50.

M-K, Gid. "Testing Testosterone Is A Waste Of Time: Delineating Gender in Sport Is Not That Easy." *Gid M-K; Health Nerd*, 4 July 2017, medium.com/@gidmk/testing-testosterone-is-a-waste-of-time-684917805957. Accessed 5 July 2017.

Magubane, Zine. "Spectacles and Scholarship: Caster Semenya, Intersex Studies, and the Problem of Race in Feminist Theory." *Signs*, vol. 39, no. 3, 2014, pp 761-85.

Magubane, Zine. "Which Bodies Matter? Feminism, Post-structuralism, Race, and the Curious Theoretical Odyssey of the 'Hottentot Venus.'" *Gender and Society*, vol. 15, no. 6, 2001, pp. 816-35.

McClintock, Anne. *Imperial Leather: Race, Gender and Sexuality in the Colonial Context*. Routledge, 1995.

McDonagh, Eileen, and Laura Pappano. Playing with Boys: Why Separate is not Equal in Sports. Oxford University Press, 2008.

Messner, Michael. *Taking the Field: Women, Men, and Sports.* University of Minnesota Press, 2002.

Miller, Patrick B. "The Anatomy of Scientific Racism: Racialist Responses to Black Athletic Achievement." *Journal of Sport History*, vol. 25, no. 1, 1998, pp. 119-51.

Mitra, Payoshni. "Male/female or other: the untold stories of female athletes with intersex variations in India." *Routledge Handbook of Sport, Gender and Sexuality*, edited by Jennifer Hargreaves and Eric Anderson, Routledge, 2014a, pp. 384-394.

Mitra, Payoshni. Interviewed by The Stream. "No Games for Women with 'too Much' Testosterone." *Aljazeera Video*, 3 Sept. 2014, stream. aljazeera.com/story/201409031709-0024124>. Accessed 14 Dec. 2015.

"Mother Insists Caster Semenya Is Not a Man." *Metro*, 21 Aug. 2009, metro.co.uk/2009/08/21/mother-insists-caster-semenya-is-not-a-man-358726/. Accessed 18 Oct. 2016.

"Mother of 800m Winner Caster Semenya Dismisses Gender Questions." *The Telegraph*, 20 Aug. 2009, www.telegraph.co.uk/sport/ othersports/athletics/6059875/Mother-of-800m-winner-Caster-Semenya-dismisses-gender-questions.html. Accessed 18 Oct. 2016.

Müller, Johannes. "Über die äusseren Geschlechtstheile der Buschmänninnen." *Archiv für Anatomie, Physiologie und wissenschaftliche Medizin*, edited by Johannes Müller, Berlin, 1834, pp. 319-45.

Munro, Brenna. "Caster Semenya: Gods and Monsters." *Safundi*, vol. 11, no. 4, 2010, pp 383-96.

"My Child Is Not a Man But a Girl." *The New Indian Express*, 20 Aug. 2009. www.newindianexpress.com/sport/2009/aug/20/my-child-is-not-a-man-but-a-girl-78996.html. Accessed 18 Oct. 2016.

Nathoo, Tasnim, and Aleck Ostry. *The One Best Way? Breastfeeding History, Politics, and Policy in Canada.* Wilfred Laurier University Press, 2009.

Nyong'o, Tavia. "The Unforgivable Transgression of Being Caster Semenya." *Women & Performance: A Journal of Feminist Theory*, vol. 20, no. 1, 2010, pp. 95-100.

O'Reilly, Andrea. *Maternal Theory.* Demeter Press, 2010.

Orr, Celeste. "(Liberatory) Reproductive Technologies and (Eugenic) Interphobic Selection."

Connecting, Rethinking and Embracing Difference, edited by Anthony Gambrell et al., Inter-disciplinary Press, 2016, pp. 87-102.

Otto, Adolf Wilhelm. *Seltene Beobachtungen zur Anatomie, Physiologie und Pathologie gehörig*. Wilibald Holäafer, 1816.

Oudshoorn, Nelly. *Beyond the Natural Body: An Archaeology of Sex Hormones*. Routledge, 1994.

Pagonis, Pidgeon. "First Do No Harm: How Intersex Kids are Hurt by Those Who Have Taken the Hippocratic Oath." *Griffith Journal of Law and Human Dignity*, vol. 5, no. 1, 2017, pp. 40-51.

Pieper, Lindsay Parks. "Sex Testing and the Maintenance of Western Femininity in International Sport." *The International Journal of the History of Sport*, vol. 31, no. 13, 2014, pp. 1557-576.

Pieper, Lindsay Parks. *Sex Testing: Gender Policing in Women's Sports*. University of Illinois Press, 2016.

Potter, Elizabeth. *Feminism and Philosophy of Science: An Introduction*. Routledge, 2006. Preves, Sharon E. "For the Sake of the Children: Destigmatizing Intersexuality." *Intersex in the Age of Ethics*, edited by Alice Domurat Dreger, University Publishing Group, 1999, pp. 51-65.

Ramsay, Michele, et al. "XX True Hermaphroditism in Southern Africa Blacks: An Enigma of Primary Sexual Differentiation." *American Journal of Human Genetics*, vol. 43, no. 1, 1988, pp. 4-13.

Reis, Elizabeth. *Bodies in Doubt: An American History of Intersex*. John Hopkins University Press, 2009.

Reis, Elizabeth. "Impossible Hermaphrodites: Intersex in America, 1620-1960." *The Journal of American History*, vol. 92, no. 2, 2005, pp. 411-41.

Roen, Katrina. "Clinical Intervention and Embodied Subjectivity: Atypically Sexed Children and their Parents." *Critical Intersex*, edited by Morgan Holmes, Ashgate Publishing Limited, 2009, pp. 15-40.

Sage, George. *Power and Ideology in American Sport*. Human Kinetics, 1998.

Schiebinger, Londa. *Nature's Body: Sexual Politics and the Making of Modern Science*. Pandora, 1993.

Schuhmann, Antje. "Taming Transgressions: South African Nation Building and 'Body Politics.' *Agenda*, vol. 24, no. 83, 2010, pp. 95-106.

"Semenym-Athletes Who Could Require Hormone Therapy to Compete." Deutsche Welle, 4 July 2017, www.dw.com/en/semenya-among-athletes-who-could-require-hormone-therapy-to-compete/a-39535753. Accessed 7 July 2017.

Simpson, Joe Leigh, et al. "Gender Verification in the Olympics." *The Journal of the American Medical Association*, vol. 284, no. 12, 2000, pp. 1568-569.

Singer, Debra S. "Reclaiming Venus: The Presence of Sarah Bartmann in Contemporary Art." *Black Venus 2010: They Called Her 'Hottentot,'* edited by Deborah Willis, Temple University Press, 2010, pp 87-95.

Somerville, Siobhan B. *Queering the Color Line: Race and the Invention of Homosexuality in American Culture*. Duke University Press, 2000.

Stoler, Ann Laura. "Making Empire Respectable: The Politics of Race and Sexual Morality in Twentieth-Century Colonial Cultures." *Dangerous Liaisons. Gender, Nation, and Postcolonial Perspectives*, edited by Anne McClintock et al., University of Minnesota Press, 1997, pp. 344-73.

Travers, Ann. "The Sport Nexus and Gender Injustice." *Studies in Social Justice*, vol. 2, no. 1, 2008, pp. 79-101.

Tourjee, Diana. "The Uncertain Olympic Future For Trans and Intersex Athletes." *Broadly*, 11 Aug. 2016, broadly.vice.com/en_us/ article/the-uncertain-olympic-future-for-trans-and-intersex-athletes. Accessed 18 Oct. 2016.

Tucker, Ross. "Hyperandrogenism and women vs women vs men in sport: A Q&A with Joanna Harper." *The Science of Sport*, 23 May 2016, sportsscientists.com/2016/05/hyperandrogenism-women-vs-women-vs-men-sport-qa-joanna-harper/. Accessed 26 Aug. 2016.

Velpeau, Alfred, A. L. M. *An Elementary Treatise on Midwifery; or, Principles of Topology and Embryology*, 3rd ed., translated by Charles D. Meigs, Lindsay and Blakiston, 1845.

Vilain, Eric. "No Clear Option for Testing; Testosterone Level Is a Start." *The New York Times*, 17 June 2012, www.nytimes.com/2012 /06/18/sports/olympics/olympic-sex-verification-you-say-youre-a-woman-that-should-be-enough.html. Accessed 12 Aug. 2016.

Viloria, Hida. "How Common is Intersex? An Explanation of the Stats." *OII-USA*, 1 Apr. 2015, oii-usa.org/2563/how-common-is-intersex-in-humans/. Accessed 21 Nov. 2016.

Viloria, Hida. "Promoting Health and Social Progress by Accepting and Depathologizing Benign Intersex Traits." *Narrative Inquiry in Bioethics*, vol. 5, no. 2, 2015, pp. 114-17.

Waitz, Theodor. *Introduction to Anthropology*. Longman, 1863.

Watson, Amanda Danielle. "Accumulating Cares: Women, Whiteness, and the Affective Labour of Responsible Reproduction in Neoliberal Times." Dissertation, University of Ottawa, 2016.

Watson, Amanda Danielle, et al. "Identity Politics and Global Citizenship in Elite Athletics: Comparing Caster Semenya and Oscar Pistorius." *Journal of Global Citizenship and Equity Education*, vol. 4, no. 1, 2014.

Willis, Deborah, editor. *Black Venus 2010: They Called her 'Hottentot.'* Temple University Press, 2010.

Wolf, Joan. *Is Breast Best? Taking on the Breastfeeding Experts and the New High Stakes of Motherhood.* New York University Press, 2010.

Yaniv, Oren. "Semenya, forced to take gender test, is a woman ... and a man." *Daily News*, 10 Sept. 2009, www.nydailynews.com/news/world/caster-semenya-forced-gender-test-woman-man-article-1.176427. Accessed 9 June 2016.

Zaccone, Laura A. "Policing the Policing of Intersex Bodies: Softening the Lines in Title IX Athletic Programs." *Brooklyn Law Review*, vol. 76, 2010, pp. 385-38.

Zeigler, Cyd. "Exclusive: Read the Olympics' new transgender guidelines that will not mandate surgery." *SB Nation Outsports*, 21 Jan. 2016, www.outsports.com/2016/1/21/10812404/transgender-ioc-policy-new-olympics. Accessed 5 Feb. 2016.

Zeitlyn, Sushila, and Rabeya Rowshan. "Privileged Knowledge and Mothers' 'Perceptions': The Case of Breast-feeding and Insufficient Milk in Bangladesh." *Medical Anthropology Quarterly*, vol. 11, 1997, pp. 56-68.

Chapter Two

Swim Coaches and Mothers: Exploring Pedagogy through Oral History

Kindell Foley Peters

Introduction

Pedagogy is the relationship among knowledge, learners, and teachers in a specific context (Armour 13-14). It is "the act of teaching together with the ideas, values and beliefs by which that act is informed, sustained and justified" (Alexander 4). Coaching pedagogy in sport has historically focused on scientific, biological, structural, or technical approaches to training (Gearity and Denison 353; Hardman and Jones 113; Lawrence et al.; Matthews et al. 70), and is a performance-based endeavour where professionals measure and quantify outcomes (Hardman and Jones 113). Performance is a dominant theme in coaching discourse and strategies based on an elite trajectory for youth sports (Ingham et al. 312); however, scholars have theorized that coaching practices should be understood socially and subjectively, since coaching decisions are not made in isolation but influenced by the personal and social context of coaches and athletes (Denison 456; Hemmestad et al. 456; Jones 168-69).

Research on coaching pedagogy has focused on the development of pedagogy or knowledge formation in general (Jones; Jones and Kingston; Jones et al.; Nelson et al.; Werthner and Trudel, "A New Theoretical"; Werthner and Trudel, "Investigating the Idiosyncratic"). Much of the scholarship on coaching focuses on elite, collegiate, or high school male coaches within team sports (Gilbert and Trudel, "Learning to Coach" 394). Most of coach learning is experiential, and coaching practice is developed from experience as an athlete and novice coach, through mentors and from continued self-learning and reflection (Gilbert and Trudel, "Analysis of Coaching" 29; Nelson et al. 253-54; Werthner and Trudel, "A New Theoretical"; Werthner and Trudel, "Investigating the Idiosyncratic"). Embodied, experiential learning in sport has been referred to as the "feel" of coaching (Hassanin and Light 3)—often unrecognized as having been formed (Light and Evans 418). A "feel" of coaching can be thought of as a personal pedagogy developed through experiences and relationships. However, few studies consider the subjective, lived experiences of women coaches, and provide little understanding of how their experiences are linked to the structural practices of sport and coaching (Norman, "Bearing the Burden" 92). Gender influences coaching performance and perceptions (Norman, "Bearing the Burden" 513, "Feeling Second Best" 95; Theberge 311-12), yet there is little research considering how gender shapes women's experiences or pedagogical and coaching choices.

Several scholars argue coaching is a form of teaching—a relationship between individuals involving a transfer of information, both physical and cognitive, which facilitates athletic skill and holistic development of the person (Gearity and Dension 355; Morgan and Sproule). Scholars have drawn links between teaching and mothering, and have indicated both are concerned about the development of children and the roles are intrinsically rewarding (Pinnegar et al. 66). Others point to how mothering and teaching offer support, guidance, and encouragement (McKenna and Wellard 281). Research on female coaches and mothering has focused on the structural challenges of being a mother and a coach (Bruening and Dixon; Kamphoff 366-7). Teri McKeever—head swim coach for the University of California Berkeley women's program and the first woman as head coach for the U.S. Olympic women's swim team—recognizes that coaching can be challenging for women. It can be difficult to blend family roles, such as marriage and children, in demanding sports careers for women who choose to make marriage or motherhood an option (Killion). She also believes her philosophy can be partially traced to her caregiving experiences as a young person (Killion). How mothering and caregiving may contribute to a coach's role, pedagogy, and philosophy needs further exploration. The purpose of this chapter is to explore the pedagogical and philosophical importance of mothering and relationships in five women's experiences as swimmers and as coaches.

The Study

The data presented here are part of a larger oral history project exploring female youth swim coaches lived experiences. The purpose of oral history is to tell someone's story to uncover the past to preserve a person's life and create "a sense of history" (Janesick 15). I define oral history as exploring how an individual stories their life to understand personal meaning of their experiences and relationships within context and what this might reveal about coaching, gender, sport, and education. Following feminist theorizing from Wanda Pillow and Patricia Leavy, I emphasize women's ways of knowing and thinking through their history, lives, and voices. Feminist oral history links women's experiences and perspectives to the contexts in which women live their lives and the thoughts and ideas that guide behaviour (Leavy 154-55). It is a way to gain personal perspective of a life lived within various sociocultural frameworks and structures.

Stories offer explanatory knowledge answering questions about how and why something happened, came to be, or developed in a particular way (Polkinghorne 11; B. Smith 91-2). I used thematic narrative analysis (Riessman 53-76) and worked inductively with the data to interpret content and identify stories and concepts. First, I considered each woman's stories independent of the other narrators, and then I looked across the women's stories for patterns (Chase 221; Luttrell 261). I used a layered account in my (re)presentation and interpretation (Goodall). Analysis focuses on the women's stories and words, with my interpretations incorporated. My own perspective as the mother of a former swimmer and involved team parent influences my interpretations. Like other feminist researchers, I accept and frame knowledge making as situated and embodied.

Methodology

I spent more than thirty hours with five female coaches discussing their life experiences as swimmers and youth swim coaches. The women were recruited through relevant snowball sampling and purposive sampling of youth swim coaches known to me through personal relationships within the swim community. Criteria for participation included past experience as a youth swimmer—at least eight years of relevant experience coaching youth—and a diverse age range to include a broad historical context. Methodology and guiding questions were based on "emergent flexible design" (Patton 43), whereby experiences in the field and inductive inquiry guide the researcher as understanding deepens and emerges, and inquiry is further concretized. In this IRB-approved study, I employed a semistructured interview guide with broad, open-ended questions allowing for a conversational style focused in a particular subject area, which enabled the conversation to progress as it may (Patton 343).

Since the study explores the life of female youth swim coaches, I met with these women over a span of days, weeks, and months to accommodate their schedules and allow dialogic space for each to narrate her experiences without feeling rushed or controlled, as well as to support inductive inquiry over time and to provide a deeper understanding of the phenomenon (Kvale 281; Minister 36; B. Smith 94). I met with each woman in their city at either their home or at a local restaurant. After these visits, Skype or FaceTime was used for subsequent meetings. During and after our conversations, I took notes, listened to the transcripts, and wrote memos, which prompted questions for our next meeting. All interviews were digitally recorded and transcribed. Each conversation session lasted anywhere from less than an hour to over two hours. Since this was a focused oral history, these women did not often speak chronologically. As a result of the circuitous nature of our conversations, the examples presented are blended from across various meetings. In addition, I removed verbal pauses, breaks, and repetitions for seamless dialogue.

The Participants

At the time of our meetings, the women ranged in age from forty-four to seventy-six and have fourteen to forty years of coaching experience in club or recreational swimming, at the collegiate level and with adult masters swimmers. Cumulatively, their swimming and coaching experiences took place in Arkansas, California, Georgia, Illinois, Indiana, Massachusetts, Montana, North Carolina, Ohio, South Carolina, Texas, and Virginia. The women are all mothers whose children ranged in age from elementary school to adult. They have sixteen children between them, and one woman currently has thirteen grandchildren and one great-grandchild. All of the women, at various points, mothered and worked fulltime in information technology, education, facilities management, and coaching. Four of the women I spoke with are currently coaching at the club level on a part-time or fulltime basis. One was also coaching high school and masters, and three were giving swimming lessons as independent business operators. One woman transitioned from being an assistant collegiate coach to supervisor of swimming and diving at a university. Four women graduated from college, and one attended for two years. At the time of our conversations, all the women were either married or widowed.

Mothering and Pedagogy

Being a woman and a mother plays a central role in their engagement as a coach on a swim team within their community. Each of the women speaks to the balancing they did or continue to do. One of the women, Chris, summed up her balancing experience as something "that comes with being a woman and a mom and a wife and coaching." Indeed, Carolyn became a coach in part to be with her children and to offer them and others an activity she enjoyed. Being a mother also helps them understand their swimmers' parents and the day-to-day struggles of getting kids fed, outfitted, and where they need to be while caring for other children and related obligations. Chris laughed while talking about her son's swim practice and her coaching occurring at the same time but in different locations: "I understand the mom's pain of trying to get different kids to different groups at practice at the same time."

Mothering directly informs these women's pedagogy. They often referred to the swimmers they currently coach as "my kids" or "my swimmers." They shared how mothering their own children helps them as a coach understand how to better communicate with children. They described themselves as mothers and coaches—role models for mothering and leading balanced lives—and, at times, contrasted themselves with male coaches whose approach or philosophy differed from their own. They described taking on a caring and nurturing role imparting life lessons and values they linked to mothering and parenting such as leadership, discipline, resilience, and respect.

Mothering Informs Coaching

"I think I've become a better coach because I'm a mom."
—Anita

Being a mother and interacting with their children everyday influences how these women communicate with and engage the swimmers. Anita discussed understanding more about daily routines, family structure, and the emotional and cognitive reactions children may have to their experiences. While reflecting on her experiences in the sport, Anita specifically indicated how much she has learned "being a woman in the sport": "I think even more so a mother. I think I've become a better coach because I'm a mom." She reinforced this belief while recalling a discussion she had with their club head coach, a male with no children: "For an age-group level and maybe even senior swimmers, I think when you're a parent there's a little bit more of understanding of words you say and situations that children are going through, through the day, that makes you more aware." This daily immersion with her children helps her improve her communication skills and be more understanding when the swimmers experience difficulties.

Carolyn, like Anita, also discussed how she is different than coaches who do not have children. She spoke about organizing practice time with discipline and structure to foster safety and maintain focus on learning. Her approach is informed by her experiences as a mother managing four children, and this approach carries over into her coaching pedagogy:

> By the time I got involved in swimming I wasn't nineteen or twenty. I was in my mid-thirties. I had four children. I think that puts you in a different frame, time of your life that you've already become disciplined because if you haven't you have children that are out of control. I had four in five and a half years so I had to be a disciplined person.

Being a mother adds valuable knowledge to the women's coaching beyond swim-skill knowledge. Anita reflected on how her own children don't always understand her and are not always willing to speak up because "they're just trying to show compliance [or] don't want to seem stupid" making her more aware of how she talks to the swimmers and work toward their better understanding. As a mother, Anita also has the opportunity to be around children in different situations—including carpools or other sport environments such as cross-country, soccer, and football—where her own children have participated. These different situations provide her with insights into other perspectives:

> Hearing them talk about things in the carpool on the way home ... things that just help, if you really listen, help you be a little, you know study that psyche a little bit more to know, ohhhhh I did that. I better not do that anymore. I then reflect and say, I remember when I said something like that one day and I didn't realize I was maybe being hurtful.

Being with children in varied contexts helps Anita reflect on her language and behavior. She described the additional layer of understanding mothering offers her as a coach:

> I just don't know if I didn't have that experience at home how I would have otherwise had that knowledge to help me interact with these children. I just think for me the experiences of my children have allowed me to really understand more how to deal with other children ... helped me be more aware of things I say or do.

Frances has learned as a mother raising her own children that "there's a fine line between being demanding and [having] expectations ...You try not to overwhelm them with your own expectations." Her approach is influenced by "being a parent and knowing what you can and can't control." She contrasted herself and a male coach she worked with years ago whose approach had an authoritarian manner she described as, "I am the coach and I'm in charge and you are to do what I am here to tell you to do." For Frances, just telling them what to do all the time is not helping them choose what works best for them. One way she does this through her pedagogy is by "respect[ing] their opinions of practice and what they're seeing and feeling" and asking them "what do you think you're gonna do differently to maybe make this better?" Encouraging them in "part of the process" is a way that she can respect them, engage them in reflective learning, and let them "think for themselves." She connected this idea to what she learned with her own children: "they've got to go through the steps how it works for them."

Chris described her approach in the following way: "I'm a mom who can help them be a better swimmer ... It [is] more of a parenting, leadership kind of role." Mothering is a leadership skill that "maintain[s] you're older than them and bring[s] them along while maintaining ... distance." Chris takes the "role in my coaching of helping guide kids in the right direction." She contrasted herself with coaches who try "to get to the kids peer-wise" and says, "that's not what I want for my kids." She described a scene she witnessed where a coach was sitting with a group of senior swimmers engaged in a conversation about another swimmer: "This one senior kid said something like, 'oh I can't stand that kid.' And then I saw the coach kinda laughing ... it bothered me." For Chris, this kind of communication is inappropriate; it does not take a leadership position or guide kids to be respectful and kind people.

For these women, their mothering informs their coaching. The experiences they have as mothers interacting day to day with their children as well as being around other children in different contexts directly influence how they communicate with the children they coach. How they communicate positions them as parents and in a leadership role. This is a way of showing and modelling respect. Being mothers provides them with skills they can transfer to the pool deck—much like how teachers indicate motherhood provides them with specific skills that can be transferred to the classroom (Reid and Miller 694).

Mothers and Coaches

"I'm more the motherly, grandmotherly influence."
— Carolyn

As mothers and coaches, they believe their purpose is to support and nurture youth's learning and abilities. Carolyn compared who she is as a coach with the behaviours she's seen from other, mostly male coaches. As a mother and a grandmother, she understands her approach as one of care, and that as a female coach, she feels she probably takes a more compassionate approach than a male: "Not that men can't be compassionate but that's just our nature." Carolyn said it was difficult for her to watch coaches who interact in disrespectful or demeaning ways: "I didn't like their demeanour with the kids. ... The way they talked at [the swimmers] ... I think they put swimmers down instead of building them up. You know, you jerk, what the hell do you think you're doing in there, type of thing. ... I just don't think that's the way to do it.

That bothers me." She said, "you should always find something positive to say to children when they get done with a swim. You want to find something positive to say to them and then maybe you have a correction." Her coaching as a mother and grandmother is to build them up—to make them feel good about their own accomplishments, feel confident, and feel good about themselves.

Helping kids feel a sense of accomplishment is a gift Anita can give a young person: "To me as a parent and as a coach that is an incredible gift that you are giving this individual for them to feel like they've accomplished something." For Anita, this role extends beyond just the swimmers she coaches. She shared a story about a young man she hired to coach for her summer recreational swim program. He stopped her after one practice to express his excitement about teaching the youth how to swim and watching them succeed. It is rewarding for Anita to have an impact on another person's life: "I left that day and I just felt like he had given me the greatest gift because I had given him the gift of getting that experience, of feeling like he had that impact on another human being." Anita connected this experience to "being a mom and loving it when my boys do something that ... [has] an impact on others." It goes beyond the satisfaction of a personal accomplishment; it is the reward of helping another person: "That's one of the reasons why I do what I do. Now it's beyond just a swimmer; it's the coaches that I'm able to impact to experience this."

Darlene's philosophy is connected to being a female role model. When reflecting on her role as a college coach for a female team, Darlene said she wanted them to see her "as a mom and a swim coach" and as having a "balanced life, too." She hoped her swimmers see her as a role model for how to be "a good mom, a good wife, and a good coach too," in much the same way as her college coach and mentor taught to her. In her coaching role, she expressed the importance of "helping them mature and learn to make ... decisions on their own" at a time when "they become women."

As mothers and coaches, they described helping the youth develop personal skills and teaching them life lessons. According to Darlene, part of coaching is "to teach them to be good human beings and responsible and respectful and hard workers.... It's little life lessons. It's parenting too." Darlene talked about how youth coaching is an extension of the mothering role. Parents are entrusting their children with her, and she's "helping mould those kids to be hard workers or to be disciplined ... to be good listeners." Frances hoped she is "developing skills within them that they can take and use later in life, away from swimming," including the importance of resilience.

Teaching them how to deal with failure is part of Frances' pedagogy and how she helps them build resilience. Rooted in her mothering experiences is her belief that children need to think, process, and try something even if she suspects it will fail. She wants to turn failure into learning or teaching moments:

> I think a lot of times today, we don't let our kids fail.... I've been guilty of it as a parent too. It's really hard as a parent to let them not do well but then what? If something goes wrong we go in and fix it for them rather than letting them come up with a solution themselves. So that's one of the things that I try to help them figure out. I'll say, "how do you want to swim [the two-hundred fly]?" They'll tell me, and I'll say, "try it that way." See how that works, and then we'll talk about it. If they screw it up, then we talk about going back and doing it another time and let's do something different.

Anita concluded that coaching is about "other character traits and other habits and that's where we go beyond just the instruction of swimming." Chris described "trying to teach them some lessons about what makes you a good friend, a good teammate." Carolyn described what she hopes to teach them through swimming: "I hope it teaches them some discipline [and] to feel good about themselves ... I'd like to think I'm building some character ... I'd like to think I'm teaching those kinds of things when I'm teaching swimming." All the women discussed how they are "teaching sportsmanship ... teamwork ... [and] how to get along with others" through swimming.

A component of these women's pedagogy is teaching personal skills through swimming such as respect, trust, leadership, perseverance, and working with others indicating broader educational objectives of community or citizenship, character and care (Gearity and Denison 355). The women want the youth to feel accomplishment and confidence in their endeavours. As mothers and coaches, they described interconnected practices supporting youth's emotional and intellectual development. For Darlene in particular, being a mother and a coach is a way to show the young women on the collegiate team that you can be successful in both roles. Mothers who are teachers also indicate the importance of being role models for young girls (Reid and Miller 697). For Carolyn, expressing compassion in coaching is natural to being a woman and a mother. This type of care reflects the idea that women's experiences can be based in "a form of caring that does not require an ethical effort" (Noddings qtd in M. Smith).

A Caring Environment

"I do the best I can when they're in my care."
— Chris

The women want to provide a positive and supportive environment, and they want the swimmers to know they care about them. For Chris, being a mother and guiding the swimmers are about imparting values of respect through caring and kindness. To do this, she invests time in getting to know the children and building relationships: "The only way to build trust is by proving yourself, that you're going to be there time and time again. You know, just by caring and showing kindness through caring. I think that models respect." Chris's coaching and mothering reflect this value: "My own children bought me something a couple of weeks ago ... if you can choose anything choose to be kind ... [so] my own personal kids hear it all the time." She transfers this value to the pool and reminds her swimmers regularly about the importance of kindness: "My kids hear me say it a lot. Like when someone gets snappy or when someone does something, I'm like, you're not being kind. Kindness and just treating everyone with respect is an important thing to me."

Prioritizing kindness and respect in her pedagogy is reflective of her mothering and helps create a safe and comfortable environment for the swimmers. For Chris, the caring ethic she has and wants for her own children is part of her pedagogy; they mutually inform each other. The caring extends beyond the pool and is a form of trust: "I want my [own] kids when they do something to go to a place where they feel safe and they can ask questions, and they can get better, and they know they're cared about by their coach. And I think my swimmers know I care more about them than just their swimming." She shared a story about a girl she coached years ago who came to her when she was struggling with personal issues: "I kinda noticed over this couple of week period ... she was just not herself. She just seemed miserable all the time.... I pulled her back [during practice], what's going on? I was grateful that I was the kind of person that she felt safe to tell me so that I could talk to her mom and help her get the help she needed." The care mothers give and want their children to receive is extended to the swim space and intertwined with their coaching.

When I asked Anita how she wanted the swimmers to think about her, the first thing she said was "someone who cares." For Anita, similar to Chris, mothering and coaching mutually inform each other: "Being a coach has helped me be a better parent ... more understanding." Coaching has enabled Anita to reflect on her parenting and how she is showing care at home and the pool: "People say, 'oh you're so patient on the pool deck,' and then I come home and I'm like ... a completely different, demanding [person]." She takes a reflective approach to understanding and improving her interactions with her biological children and the children she coaches:

> Am I being as good of a parent as I am a coach and am I being as good of a coach as I am as a parent? You know both ways. The things I have to work on working with children in both venues, am I equally diligent in applying the good skills or characteristics in each endeavour?

All the women described the importance of getting to know the swimmers individually both on the pool deck and off in order to understand the best ways to motivate them, develop approaches for teaching them, and help them balance and manage the pressures they may face. Darlene discussed how her approach needs to change depending on the child she is helping: "[You] gotta figure out all those little idiosyncrasies and try to go with them. Mould; change your ways to help them be the best they can be." Darlene provided examples, representing similar stories expressed by all the women, of being observant and sharing experiences as a way to understand the youth better. "I get to know them through the day, ins and outs. You know sometimes when they're walking in that they had a bad day just by the way they're carrying themselves." She added, "The only way to learn that is to get to know the kids through interactions at practice, on the deck, [and] maybe having team dinners or team functions." She also tries to be available and supportive when they need help: "I remember some kids would have flashcards, and sometimes I would quiz them in between sets or something like that if they had a big test coming up and they asked me to help them."

The women want to provide a supportive and caring environment reflective of what Nel Noddings refers to as caring relations in education. They described being attentive, listening, and trying to understand the needs of the youth they coach. This is in keeping with other scholars who describe female coaches' style as caring and understanding (Fasting and Pfister 103). They shared examples of modelling and demonstrating care in their interactions and relations with the youth they coach. Noddings believes this is part of an educator's responsibility. They also described an aspect of their coaching is providing support and guidance, an approach echoed in research on mothering and classroom teaching (McKenna and Wellard 281). Teaching respect through mothering as a pedagogical approach extends understanding of women's coaching values described in team sports (Callary et al.).

Conclusion

To guide others, teachers must be aware of their histories or herstories, how their experiences and relationships contribute to those stories, and how they contribute to their pedagogical choices (Costandi). The same can be argued for coaches. Most of coach learning is experiential and personal. For these women coaches, their "feel" of coaching is in many ways connected to what they've learned through their experiences as mothers. They described guiding the swimmers to develop such values as kindness, respect, resilience, hard work, discipline, and responsibility, often connecting this guidance with mothering. They embody their roles as mothers and coaches, and their experiences provide a glimpse into how their history as mothers and coaches has shaped their pedagogical choices.

Swimming pedagogical practices have been described as disciplinary physiological practices, in which the body is a commodity and an instrument to be manipulated to improve performance (McMahon and DinanThompson 42). Swim coaching scholarship points to developing efficient and correct technique through direct instruction such as talk and demonstration, monitoring movement, and engaging the mind to connect language, movement, and sensation (Light and Wallian 392-93; Peters 28). All the women described how their first pedagogical objective is teaching youth to be better swimmers and how they strive to improve their coaching abilities. However, the women's stories rarely focused on detailed strategies they used for developing stroke technique or physical conditioning, achieving performance goals, or meeting swim time-based benchmarks. Their stories and memories emphasized pedagogy aimed at developing young people in addition to developing good stroke mechanics and techniques. Much of what these women described in their interactions and relations with their young swimmers reflects what Nell Noddings describes as a relational sense of caring. The approach they described taking as women and mothers is in contrast to authoritarian, autocratic, or masculine styles of communicating and interacting that have been used to describe some male coaches (Fasting and Pfister 103; Tomlinson and Yourganci 143).

The women expressed an investment in the swimmers and a connection they believe helps them better communicate, teach, and guide them. They described a relationship that lets the children know the coaches care about them as more than just a swimming body. Through swimming, they hope to teach the youth skills and habits they can apply throughout their lives. Previous interviews with women swim coaches also speak to a caring pedagogy, which transcends the pool (Peters 28). As Anita said, "[I am] proud that I'm able to send them out into this work world knowing that I've contributed to the health and the personal feeling of success of a lot of these swimmers." The coaches showed joy when discussing their former swimmers' successes beyond youth swimming, especially in other areas of their life. They shared letters, notes, and stories with me from past swimmers they coached that expressed gratitude and thankfulness for their support, encouragement, and life lessons. These are intrinsic rewards to mothering and coaching, which are similar to the rewards scholars have described for mothering and teaching (Pinnegar et al. 66). Chris summed it up beautifully: "It's not just swimming for me. I like watching them grow and become these amazing people."

Works Cited

Alexander, Robin. *Essays on Pedagogy*. Routledge, 2008.

Armour, Kathleen. "What is 'Sport Pedagogy' and Why Study it?" *Sport Pedagogy: An Introduction for Teaching and Coaching*, edited by Kathleen Armour, Routledge, 2011, pp. 11-24.

Bruening, Jennifer E., and Marlene A. Dixon. "Situating Work-family Negotiations within a Life Course Perspective: Insights on the Gendered Experiences of NCAA Division I Head Coaching Mothers." *Sex Roles*, vol. 58, 2008, pp. 10-23.

Callary, Bettina et al. "Exploring Coaching Actions Based on Developing Values: A Case Study of a Female Hockey Coach." *International Journal of Lifelong Education*, vol. 32, no. 2, 2013, pp. 209-29.

Chase, Susan E. "Narrative Inquiry: Multiple Lenses, Approaches, Voices." *Qualitative Educational Research: Readings in Reflexive Methodology and Transformative Practice*, edited by Wendy Luttrell, Routledge, 2010, pp. 208-36.

Costandi, Samia. *Between Middle East and West: Exploring the Experience of a Palestinian-Canadian Teacher Through Narrative Inquiry*. Dissertation, McGill University, 2006.

Denison, Jim. "Planning, Practice and Performance: The Discursive Formation of Coaches' Knowledge. "*Sport, Education and Society*, vol. 15, no. 4, 2010, pp. 461-78.

Fasting, Kari, and Gertrud Pfister. "Female and Male Coaches in the Eyes of Female Elite Soccer Players." *European Physical Education Review*, vol. 6, no. 1, 2000, pp. 91-110.

Gearity, Brian T., and Jim Denison. "Educator-Coach as Stranger." *Cultural Studies-Critical Methodologies*, vol. 12, no. 4, 2012, pp. 352-6.

Gilbert, Wade D., and Pierre Trudel "Analysis of Coaching Science Research Published from 1970-2001." *Research Quarterly for Exercise and Sport*, vol. 75, no. 4, 2004, pp. 388-99.

Gilbert, Wade D., and Pierre Trudel. "Learning to Coach Through Experience: Reflection in Model Youth Sport Coaches." *Journal of Teaching in Physical Education*, vol. 21, 2001, pp. 16-34.

Goodall Jr., H.L. *Writing Qualitative Inquiry: Self, Stories, and Academic Life*. Left Coast Press, Inc., 2008.

Hardman, Alun, and Carwyn Jones. "Ethics for Coaches." In *An Introduction to Sports Coaching: Connecting Theory to Practice*. 2nd ed., edited by Robyn L. Jones and Kieran Kingston, pp. 113-30. Routledge, 2013.

Hassanin, Remy, and Light, Richard L. "The Use of Habitus in Research on Experience and Coach Development." Joint AARE APERA International Conference, Dec. 2012, Sydney, Australia. www1.aare. edu.au/papers/2012/Hassanin%20R.pdf#zoom=85.

Hemmestad, Liv B., et al. "Phronetic Social Science: A Means of Better Researching and Analysing Coaching?" *Sport, Education and Society*, vol. 15, no. 4, 2010, pp. 447-59.

Ingham, Alan G., et al. "From the Performance Principle to the Developmental Principle: Every Kid a Winner?" *Quest*, vol. 54, 2002, pp. 308-31.

Janesick, Valerie J. *Oral History for the Qualitative Researcher: Choreographing the Story*. Guilford Press, 2010.

Jones, Robyn. "Coaching Redefined: An Everyday Pedagogical Endeavor." *Sport, Education and Society*, vol. 12, no. 2, 2007, pp. 159-73.

Jones, Robyn, et al. "Developing Coaching Pedagogy: Seeking a Better Integration of Theory and Practice. "*Sport, Education and Society*, vol. 17, no. 3, 2012, pp. 313-29.

Jones, Robyn L., and Kieran Kingston. *An Introduction to Sports Coaching: Connecting Theory to Practice*. 2nd ed., Routledge, 2013.

Kamphoff, Cindra S. "Bargaining with Patriarchy: Former Female Coaches' Experiences and Their Decision to Leave Collegiate Coaching." *Research Quarterly for Exercise and Sport*, vol. 81, no. 3, 2010, pp. 360-72.

Killion, Ann. "McKeever Blazes New Trail as First Female Coach of U.S. Swimming." *Sports Illustrated*, 25 June 2012, www.si.com/more-sports/2012/06/25/teri-mckeever-2012-us-olympic-swimming-trials. Accessed 7 Feb 2017.

Kvale, Steinar. "The 1,000-page Question." *Qualitative Inquiry*, vol. 2, no. 3, 1996, pp. 275-84.

Lawrence, Gavin et al. "Skill Acquisition for Coaches." In *An Introduction to Sports Coaching: Connecting Theory to Practice*. 2nd ed., edited by Robyn L. Jones and Kieran Kingston, pp. 31-46. Routledge, 2013.

Leavy, Patricia L. "The Practice of Feminist Oral History and Focus Group Interviews." *Feminist Research Practice*, edited by Sharlene Nagy Hesse-Biber and Patricia L. Leavy, Sage, 2007, pp. 149-86.

Light, Richard L., and John Robert Evans. "Dispositions of Elite-level Australian Rugby Coaches towards Game Sense: Characteristics of Their Coaching Habitus." *Sport, Education and Society*, vol. 18, no. 3, 2013, pp. 407-23.

Light, Richard, and Nathalie Wallian. "A Constructivist-informed Approach to Teaching Swimming." *Quest*, vol. 60, 2008, pp. 387-404.

Luttrell, Wendy. "'Good Enough' Methods for Life-story Analysis." *Qualitative Education Research*, edited by Wendy Luttrell, Routledge, 2010, pp. 258-78.

Matthews, Nic, et al. "Sociology for Coaches." In *An Introduction to Sports Coaching: Connecting Theory to Practice*. 2nd ed., edited by Robyn L. Jones and Kieran Kingston, pp. 69-80. Routledge, 2013.

McKenna, Lisa, and Sally Wellard. "Mothering: An Unacknowledged Aspect of Undergraduate Clinical Teachers' Work in Nursing." *Advances in Health Science Education*, vol. 14, no. 2, 2008, pp. 275-85.

McMahon, Jenny, and Maureen DinanThompson. "'Body Work-regulation of a Swimmer Body': An Autoethnography from an Australian Elite Swimmer." *Sport, Education and Society*, vol. 16, no. 1, 2011, pp. 35-50.

Minister, Kristina. "A Feminist Frame for the Oral History Interview." *Womens Words: The Feminist Practice of Oral History*, edited by Sherna Berger Gluck and Daphne Patai, Routledge, 1991, pp. 27-41.

Morgan, Kevin and John Sproule. "Pedagogy for Coaches." In *An Introduction to Sports Coaching: Connecting Theory to Practice*. 2nd ed., edited by Robyn L. Jones and Kieran Kingston, pp. 15-30. Routledge, 2013.

Nelson, Lee J., et al. "Formal, Nonformal and Informal Coach Learning: A Holistic Conceptualisation." *International Journal of Sports Sciences & Coaching*, vol. 1, no. 3, 2006, pp. 247-59.

Noddings, Nel. "Caring in Education." *Infed*, www.infed.org/mobi/caring-in-education. Accessed 30 Jan 2017.

Norman, Leanne. "Bearing the Burden of Doubt: Women Coaches' Experiences of Gender Relations." *Research Quarterly for Exercise and Sport*, vol. 81, 2010, pp. 506-17.

Norman, Leanne. "Feeling Second Best: Elite Women Coaches' Experiences." *Sociology of Sport Journal*, vol. 27, 2010, pp. 89-104.

Patton, Michael Quinn. *Qualitative Research & Evaluation Methods*. 3rd ed., Sage, 2002.

Peters, Kindell F. "Pedagogical Practices of Swim Coaches." Society for Educating Women Annual Conference, Sep 2012, St. Louis, Missouri. Conference Presentation.

Pillow, Wanda S. "Gender Matters: Feminist Research in Educational Evaluation." *New Directions for Evaluation*, vol. 96, 2002, pp. 9-26.

Pinnegar, Stefinee, et al. "Teaching as Highlighted by Mothering: A Narrative Inquiry." *Studying Teacher Education*, vol. 1, no. 1, 2005, pp. 55-67.

Polkinghorne, Donald E. "Narrative Configuration in Qualitative Analysis." *Life History and Narrative*, edited by J. Amos Hatch and Richard Wisniewski, Falmer Press, 1995, pp. 5-23.

Reid, Julie A., and Amy Chasteen Miller. "'We Understand Better Because We Have Been Mothers': Teaching, Maternalism, and Gender Equality in Bolivian Education." *Gender and Education,* vol. 26, no. 6, 2014, pp. 688-704.

Riessman, Catherine Kohler. *Narrative Methods for the Human Sciences*. Sage, 2008.

Smith, Brett. "Narrative Inquiry: Ongoing Conversations and Questions for Sport and Exercise Psychology Research." *International Review of Sport and Exercise Psychology,* vol. 3, no. 1, 2010, pp. 87-107.

Smith, Mark K. "Nel Noddings, the Ethics of Care and Education." *Infed* www.infed.org/mobi/nel-noddings-the-ethics-of-care-and-education/. Accessed 30 Jan 2017.

Theberge, Nancy. "The Construction of Gender in Sport: Women, Coaching, and the Naturalization of Difference." *Social Problems,* vol. 40, no. 3, 1993, pp. 301-13.

Tomlinson, Alan, and Ilkay Yorganci. "Male Coach / Female Athlete Relations: Gender and Power Relations in Competitive Sport." *Journal of Sport & Social Issues,* vol. 21, 1997, pp. 134-55.

Werthner, Penny, and Pierre Trudel. "A New Theoretical Perspective for Understanding How Coaches Learn to Coach." *The Sport Psychologist,* vol. 20, 2006, pp. 198-212.

Werthner, Penny, and Pierre Trudel. "Investigating the Idiosyncratic Learning Paths of Elite Canadian Coaches." *International Journal of Sports Science & Coaching,* vol. 4, no. 3, 2009, pp. 433-49.

Chapter 3

Quit Calling My Kid Yao Ming: Reflections of Race and Class from a Chinese Basketball Mom

Catherine Ma

The impact of two iconic basketball players in the National Basketball Association (NBA)—Yao Ming and Jeremy Lin—has been a driving force in challenging stereotypes of Asian and Asian American men, which highlights race in a whole new way on the basketball court. As numerous articles and films have documented the physical and psychological challenges they faced, the presence of these two athletes offers us a unique perspective in how we look at the intersections between race and class in sports.

In this chapter, I engage with these intersections through my experience as a Chinese basketball mom whose son plays Amateur Athletic Union (AAU), or travel basketball, in the tristate New York area, and Catholic Youth Organization (CYO) basketball. Through the disciplinary lenses of spectator, mother, psychologist, and researcher, I explore how race and class on the basketball court challenges yet keeps static stereotypes of Asian and Asian American masculinity and their subsequent effects on mothering.

My Most Important Mothering Lesson

As a Chinese mother, there have been times when I have failed, but I try to look upon these transgressions as ways to expand my mothering skills. One such incident was when I deemed the rest of the players on the team to be exerting much more effort than my own son, which led me to criticize his lack of effort, resulting in his tears. I felt I had slowly turned into the main character in Amy Chua's book, *Battle Hymn of the Tiger Mom*, which refers to strictness in mothering and is considered stereotypical of many Asian mothers. Tears to a Tiger Mom is like pouring gasoline on a fire, and incited me to angrily ask, "Why are you even crying?" His tearful reply was that basketball should be fun, and at that moment, it dawned on me that he was correct. Basketball should be fun, and I was in the wrong. To make matters worse, he was only ten or eleven at the time, but in my head, I had expectations of him training like Jeremy Lin. Amanda Visek and colleagues have found that the integration of "fun" is vital in sports participation and longevity when it came to children pursuing sports (431). Unfortunately, parental goals of winning and teaching their children how not to accept mediocrity tend to be misaligned with children's goals, which focus on the simplicity of having fun while they engage in sports. I expected this little ten-year-old boy to train like a professional NBA player, and it was difficult for me to see how this view often trumped the fun of playing basketball. Fortunately, I found that my own conceptions of being a Chinese mother were limiting how I viewed my son's talent and effort. This epiphany highlighted the irony of my own biases when it came to the work ethic of Chinese people. I was forcing it on him as a way to motivate him to excel among his teammates, but I was unaware that this pressure often took the fun out of basketball and made him less likely to exert effort. I had unknowingly internalized the model minority myth that Chinese people have to give double, if not triple, the amount of work, dedication, and practice if we are to be accepted into American culture and be upwardly mobile (Wu 243, 253). Since that conversation, I have learned to be a better spectator and less judgmental in evoking unrealistic and unreasonable expectations, which Eriberto Lozada finds common among nonathletes, such as myself (223). My son taught me a valuable lesson that day and helped me see my own biases in mothering the athlete in him. There have been numerous times when I mentioned to him that it would be okay if he wanted to quit his school's CYO team and focus more on travel basketball, but he always chose to stay on that team and play with his classmates—even though I found the coaching and refereeing to be subpar and riddled with nepotism. I am starting to realize that the fun factor is something that he values over winning, and I am slowly accepting his decision that his balancing of winning and having fun is probably more accurate than mine. As I attend more travel tournaments with my son, I am beginning to realize that my experiences as a Chinese basketball mom are much more than simply basketball games. Each game has given me numerous opportunities to learn about myself and better understand how others react to me and my son based on our race, ethnicity, and class. Some experiences have been pleasant, whereas others have been less so, but I strongly believe that these experiences can help make salient the racial and class issues underlining youth basketball and foster new ways to increase inclusivity and diversity in all youth sports.

The neoliberalization of youth sports is creating a dynamic that tends to focus primarily on winning. It seems as though the days of unstructured play are gone, when children's playing focused on aspects of team building, inclusion, fitness, and simply having fun. There is a growing gap between unstructured and competitive play. Youth sports teams often entail stringent tryouts that further seek to separate children across class, sex, race, and ethnic divides. With their emphasis on equality and equity, theories of social justice reveal how organized team sports and physical education are used to maintain the status quo in social inequalities (Dagkas 222). This view has enhanced victim blaming. Health is viewed as agentic and a choice, whereas blame and shame are heaped upon those who do not make it to the wellness finish line. The individual is responsible for wellbeing versus the collective.

As a result, individuals considered unhealthy, overweight, or obese are viewed as lazy, uneducated, or hedonistic. What critics do not take into account is how some neighbourhoods are food deserts, where healthy produce is unavailable or communities are crime-ridden, making it unsafe for outdoor exercise or play (Dagkas 223). These findings point to the significance of class distinctions when it comes to who is afforded the opportunity to participate and reap the health benefits of team sports.

The Impact of Class on Team Sports

The importance of creating an inclusive atmosphere for all children regarding sports is gaining momentum with the health initiative sponsored by the Aspen Institute with Project Play, which aims to take a unified approach to assure that all children ages twelve and under, regardless of their race, ethnicity, or socioeconomic status, have access to the benefits of team sports. Results from their 2015 report–*Sport for All, Play for Life: A Playbook to Get Every Kid in the Game*—found that a family's household income was a strong deciding factor in determining an early entry point into team sports (7). Indeed, children from wealthier households were almost 50 percent more likely to engage in team sports as compared to their less affluent peers. Having attended public school and living in a low-income neighbourhood as a child, I was struck by the class distinctions in AAU and CYO sports. Participating in a team was foreign to me because my parents never had the finances for me to play a sport, nor did it dawn on me that public elementary schools did not offer team sports until high school. This disparity can create an unfair advantage where children attending private elementary schools have multiple opportunities to practice their chosen sport or multiple sports, whereas children attending public schools can only participate in team sports when they enter high school. Children who live in households with annual incomes of $25,000 or less were about 50 percent less likely to participate in sports as compared with those from households with incomes of $100,000 or more (The Aspen Institute 7). In the long run, this difference may affect their ability to secure sports scholarships for college, widening the gap between classes. For some parents, having their child receive a sports scholarship may be the only way they can afford college, which puts a lot of pressure on the child's athletic abilities and ability to perform on the court. Sohaila Shakib et al. support this finding, as lower socioeconomic status male youths often have fewer opportunities outside of sports to attend college as compared to their more affluent peers who have more options afforded to them (307). Outside of school, I have also noticed how these class differences extended to activities over the summer.

Ever since my son was in third grade, he has spent a few weeks of his summer break attending a variety of basketball camps. It was during his second summer at basketball camp that one of the camp's coaches asked him to join his travel team. This was how we became introduced to travel basketball, which helped improve his game and exposed him to a wider range of tournaments in the tristate area. As he began to outgrow that initial basketball camp, which was more family friendly and nurturing, he gravitated toward other camps more focused on skills training and geared to older boys. These basketball camps are considered huge moneymakers for the owners—tuition starts around $300 to over $1,000 per week—and fertile scouting grounds for high school and travel basketball coaches to recruit players for their teams. Gaining access to these basketball camps requires significant finances and time. This can further widen the gap between young people's engagement with team sports and their overall physical health—including reductions in adult obesity, greater self-esteem, less likely to engage in risky behaviours, higher educational aspirations, greater likelihood to attend college, and increased income potential (The Aspen Institute 5; Marsh 215). Families who have limited financial means do not gain access to these benefits, nor do they get access to AAU sports, teams that start in elementary school, facilities to practice in, or coaches who are actually paid a salary to coach young athletes.

The travel teams that are more difficult to beat are usually from wealthier neighbourhoods because they have access to all the aforementioned freedoms and benefits. The majority of parents who put their children in travel basketball often have the financial stability to pay for costly registration fees, out of state tournaments, overnight lodging, meals, uniforms, personal trainers, and equipment. They also have the ability to have at least one parent commit their time to bringing their athletes to practices and games. I have noticed that many of my son's teammates have either a stay-at-home mother and/or a father with a flexible work schedule who can drop off their children and pick them up. I am fortunate that being in academe, I do have flexibility in my teaching schedule and can decide whether or not to teach over the summer to accommodate my children's schedules. Families struggling to pay the bills or working multiple jobs to just survive may not have the extra resources for their children to attend these camps, often creating an unfair advantage on and off the basketball court. As a result, there is less diversity when it comes to who gets to attend these basketball camps. The needs of disadvantaged children who could reap the benefits of attending these camps are often ignored making initiatives such as Project Play by the Aspen Institute or research in social justice education, all the more critical in challenging these inequities in health pedagogies and youth sports as they identify the needs of Black and ethnic minority youth (Dagkas 221). It is hopeful that systemic changes are being discussed by major advocacy organizations, such as the Aspen Institute, as this is a much-needed starting point in addressing discriminatory practices in basketball.

Discriminatory Practices in Basketball

Having Yao Ming inducted into the Basketball Hall of Fame and Jeremy Lin playing for the Atlanta Hawks are significant game changers, as these two athletes are teaching the world about covert and overt discrimination in the NBA. At the beginning of the movie *Linsanity*, Lin is stopped by security officers at the players entrance and asked if he belongs with the team. This is a perfect example that illustrates how the Asian American athlete is still seen as an anomaly. Although Lin does not dwell on this blatant disrespect, these daily microaggressions can contribute to stress among Asian Americans, which can often increase their levels of stress and negative health outcomes (Ong 192). On the other hand, Yao and Lin are teaching us a new side to Asian male stereotypes—one that forces us to reexamine our own beliefs regarding Asian male masculinity and athletic prowess, while challenging societal views when it comes to stereotypes that normalize white and Black bodies in sports (Thangaraj 136). As a result, we are seeing more Asians and Asian Americans joining together to call out egregious behaviours and blatant discrimination against them. During the 2004-2005 NBA playoffs between the Houston Rockets and the Dallas Mavericks, Yao was called for a series of "phantom fouls." Referees called excessive fouls against his moving screens, which ignited the role of race and ethnicity in racially charged calls (Farred 1). Grant Farred has argued that the Asian player bears an unnecessary vulnerability to certain referee calls that Black players do not have to contend with, which is a covert form of racism on the court (28). His assumptions may not be too farfetched, as the Rocket's coach at that time, Jeff Van Gundy, was punished with one of the most severe fines in NBA history for suggesting that the league office was instructing referees to single out Yao's moving screens (Farred 27). The severity of the fine is an effective deterrent, and implies that the NBA has carte blanche on any coach who questions its authority.

Calling excessive fouls is one half of the problem, whereas ignoring and refusing to call fouls is the other. Hsiu-Chen Kuei, a mother from California, created a video comprised of fouls committed on Lin, and sent it to the NBA asking them to review the footage. The fouls appeared to be flagrant ones, which occur from unnecessary physical contact to an opponent's head area and can result in great physical harm to the player (Jeremy Lin: Too Flagrant Not to Call; NBA Video Rulebook). Her video went viral with close to two million hits, resulting in several Asian and Asian American activist groups writing the NBA and alleging that there was preferential treatment for players who committed flagrant fouls against Lin, since the offenses were purposely ignored. The NBA offered this statement: "After reviewing our extensive officiating database, we have found no data that suggests Jeremy Lin is disadvantaged by our officiating staff." (NBA Official). Based on the NBA's apathetic response, Asian American groups were outraged and rallied to support Lin citing discrimination against Asian American players. The dismissive response of the NBA may be related to the view of Asian American athletes as weak, fragile, and nonconfrontational; they, thus, do not belong in a physically dominating sport such as professional basketball (Thangaraj 136). Based on these stereotypes, fouls against Asian American athletes are not likely to be called by the referees as a means to discourage their sense of belonging in the NBA while encouraging them to "man up" and play more aggressively. This view of "manning up" and playing aggressively was also a factor in Yao's initial style of play, which was criticized as being too soft and nonphysical. It was viewed as a detriment to the Houston Rockets because it made him vulnerable to bad calls by the referees (Farred 60-61). To resolve this situation, the Rockets coach hired Moses Malone to toughen Yao up so he would become accustomed to the physical contact, and in essence, to make him play more like a Black center (Farred 61). Rather than embrace a multiplicity of basketball playing styles, the NBA and its coaches resorted to a single aggressive style of play with no room for alternatives. Seeing how Asian and Asian American basketball players seemed to be found on the opposite ends of the spectrum when it came to either having fouls ignored or being called excessively for fouls, I noticed how my son also fell on both sides of the continuum. He was excessively called for fouls for no other reason than being taller and bigger than the average ten-year-old and being Chinese, whereas fouls against him were often ignored.

In the majority of his CYO games, I noticed that the referees often called fouls on my son, yet they ignored the same fouls from opposing players who were not as tall. During one game, he became annoyed when he had a foul called on him while both his hands were straight up in the air, as he used his body to block his opponent. When he questioned why was he fouled, the referee replied that he could not use his body to block, which is completely false as using your body is the correct way to block an opponent. In many ways, he is being subjected to Farred's term "phantom fouls," also known as a form of discriminatory practice that singles out particular players. In our case, it was for the simple fact that he is the tallest and most talented Asian athlete in his age category of the entire CYO league (1). Challenging the discriminatory view that only a certain type of athlete can succeed in basketball makes many people uncomfortable. In our situation, many referees con-sistently target my son with absurd calls. The example I offered is just one of many questionable decisions by the referees against my son, but to expose the effects of race and class in youth basketball is one way to counter these discriminatory acts. What infuriates me about these calls, other than being incorrect, is that they send the wrong message to the opposing team: they can purposefully hard foul my son without any consequences. It also promotes the belief that only players of a certain race or ethnicity belong in CYO sports.

This bias by CYO referees is obvious. On multiple occasions, they have approached my husband and me after the game to explain that because of our son's size, they have to call these fouls on him. One referee disclosed to us that they "had to" call these fouls on him because he will likely be called on them when he reaches high school. This made absolutely no logical sense as they were not high school referees nor was this a high school game, yet they felt they were doing us a favor by sharing their faulty logic with us. A deeper analysis of the referees' calls indicates their refusal to acknowledge that a Chinese boy can be over six feet tall and a good athlete. Consequently, the only power these referees have to repudiate these facts is to equalize the height advantage of my son by calling ridiculous fouls against him while turning a blind eye to the same fouls committed against him. I have loudly expressed my irritation at these referees, which has resulted in threats of being thrown out of the game or suspended from multiple games for voicing my concern. I am also equally angered by the lack of support from my son's coaches because their silence acts as compliance.

Critics of the NBA's response to Kuei's video have noted that denial of Lin's possible flagrant fouls sends a negative message to children because it condones this behaviour and fails to protect the players (Lee). As a mother to an athlete, I find many mothers get upset when their children get hurt during the game—not through accidents on the court but as a result of egregious contact and unsportsmanlike behaviour. Discriminatory behaviour, microaggressions, and macroaggressions are not just targeted toward players, as I have witnessed times when parents and coaches were also guilty of such behaviours when we played against teams that were racially homogenous.

Playing Racially Homogenous Teams

One weekend, we played two teams that left an indelible impression on me. One was a travel team from Buffalo, New York, whose players and coaches were all Black, as were the referees. Sitting next to one of the moms from this team, I asked her how old the players were on her team, and she told me they were fourteen and under. Their team was much faster, taller, quicker, and more experienced than ours. Although we have some excellent outside shooters, we were a team comprised of twelve-year-olds, and no match for this older team. We were down by twenty points, and the opposing coach told his players to go easy on us as to not drive the score any higher. Upon hearing this, a father on our team to express his displeasure at that coach's instructions because he wanted our team to play against their team at full force. He did not want any mercy because we drove an hour to play against them, and from his point of view, the only way to improve our game was to play more advanced teams. Out of all the travel tournaments in our age bracket, we had been undefeated, which prompted our coaches to sign up for tournaments against older teams. Words were exchanged between that father on our team and the opposing coach. Their disagreement prompted one referee to say "I want to kick that father's ass." and the opposing coach responded with, "Leave the coaching up to me so I can destroy their team." Sitting on the bleachers with the opposing team made me privy to many of the disturbing comments and gave me new insight on how the sidelines operate. These arguments are not uncommon in youth sports with many games being played as if they were the NBA championships.

What I found troublesome was how the father from our team escalated the situation by going to complain to the owner of the establishment who was Caucasian. I observed them chatting and laughing out loud as if they were longtime buddies. This act can be construed as a microaggression to people of colour and tends to increase the racial tension on the court. The mere fact that the father on our team chose to speak with the owner of the establishment, who is of the same or similar race, can be construed as an act of aggression, as the owner did not come to over to the Black coach to alleviate any racial tension or misunderstanding. There was no joking or camaraderie toward the Black coach or Black fathers. Is it discriminatory to only converse with the father on our team and not the Black coach or Black fathers? After witnessing this behaviour, I can understand why some Black teams may feel uneasy when these side conversations occur in their presence and when they do not have the same camaraderie extended to them.

The second team we played was from CYO, and they were an all-Asian team, including their coaches. Of all the teams we have played against, I have noticed that many Asian teams have a strong desire to win at all costs and will often play excessively rough while exhibiting unsportsmanlike conduct. There was one parish team whose coach would purposefully make noises to distract our players during free throws. One of the fathers from our team played on a men's basketball league with that coach and noted that he would behave in a similar manner during their adult matches. The offensive behavior of this coach comprised of clapping his hands loudly and whistling like a bird in an attempt to distract our players during their free throws. Even the referee asked him to stop what he was doing, but he continued to the point where I shouted across the court to tell him to stop whistling, as he denied any unsportsmanlike behaviour on his part. It was a close game, and whenever his team scored, he would clap extra loud, or when we had the ball, he would scream "defense" as loud as he could. When fouls were called on our players, he would shout out the number of fouls our players had accumulated. I had never witnessed such unsportsmanlike and annoying behaviour from any team, whether it was travel or CYO. Our team and families have never been one to initiate such behaviour, but after multiple requests to cease to no avail, we decided to mirror his behavior. As that team clapped loudly, we also clapped just as loud to the point where the referee had to remind both teams that this is Catholic Youth Organization basketball and that we should behave like better Catholics. Another heated argument ensued between the opposing coaches and the fathers on our team resulting in the whistling coach yelling out loud that we were sore losers even though we won that game. Angry words were continually exchanged between the coaches and the fathers afterward. My son shared how one of his opponents expressed his embarrassment over his coach's behaviour because the kids just wanted to play basketball. I find this is often the case when players on the court merely want to play ball and do not want to be involved in all the disagreements occurring off court. The results of this game reminded me of a different travel game when we also played against another all-Asian team—a game that highlighted to me the psychological aspects of parenting in basketball.

Psyching Yourself Up and Out in Basketball

We played another all-Asian team, which was comprised of much older and skilled AAU players. They had won the previous two tournaments with ease, and after witnessing their ability on the court, I was not sure if our team could beat them. They started off very strong, but we were able to catch up before halftime. As a result, their team became easily exasperated as one of their key players said they needed a center, as they could not win with only guards on the court. After we caught up to tie the game, the self-confidence of the opposing team began to wane, as they exhibited increased frustration. Sherri Grasmuck explains that teams whose players turn on one another tend to crack under the intensity of certain games and are less resilient after setbacks, even though they may be more skilled than their opponents (199). It seemed as though this team was unfamiliar with having a team catch up, tie up the score, and surpass them. We won that game by a few points, and it was clear that they lost their momentum once we caught up to them. When doubt crept into their minds, it became easier to beat them, which highlights the psychological component of basketball.

As a social-personality psychologist and mother, I have noticed some interesting differences from observing how various teams play. I find the all-Asian teams to have an intense desire to win and have a significant amount of familial support present. My observations find a distinct difference in the psychological side of youth basketball. Asian players, for example, begin psyched up to win and play hard. They start out strong, but when the opposing team catches up and figures out a successful defensive strategy, the loud support of their parents dwindles, and the players' performance wanes. It seems as though the waning support was their Achilles heel or weak spot, and the resultant effects were their game becoming sloppier, and the players becoming easily frustrated. Their teamwork begins to crumble just enough for the opposing team to defeat them.

On the other hand, I have noticed a different dynamic with all-Black teams. There are fewer parents in the stands to cheer them on; however, when they are down and losing, these players often work even harder to psych themselves up. Their coaches yell and scream at them, and they will use that as motivation to step up their game. Sometimes we can beat those teams, but other times, their drive to win overpowers us, and we end up losing. These differences in outcome may be connected to parenting style. The Asian parenting style I observed seemed harsh— affection and support were tied to their child's performance level. If their child excelled on the court, there was great outward affection and cheering, but when their performance was low, the Asian parents would withdraw their affection and become silent. When the Asian players were scoring well, there was a lot of clapping from their parents and overt support, but when their team began to lose, there was often silence on the spectator side. Players would notice this change, and it would chip away at their self-confidence. On the other hand, when the Black teams were doing well, there was less cheering, but when they started to lose, there were harsh words regarding their performance from the few parents and coaches. These harsh words served to motivate their players. They would drive the team to play harder to ultimately win the game. My roles as spectator, psychologist, researcher, and mother allow me to see these differences that may not seem significant to other parents, and such differences in viewpoint present unique challenges in how I mother my son.

Unique Challenges in Mothering an Athlete

When it comes to mothering an athlete, I feel I have a great responsibility to raise a young man who understands his boundaries both on and off the court. It is of utmost importance for me to teach him self-respect so that he can develop self-respect for others. Understanding what consent means, that "no" means no, are important life lessons that often don't seem to apply to white male athletes such as David Becker and Brock Turner (Hauser). Young athletes need to know so much more than merely playing a game. Today's social climate for these young men and women is more complicated than it was decades ago, but these complexities offer parents a great opportunity to discuss with our children the misogyny that often comprises the dark side of sports. I do know that parents play a crucial role in shaping the next generation of male athletes to be kinder and more respectful to not only themselves but to others, and this can be transformative to both parent and child. Unfortunately, some believe that these characteristics are not compatible with playing in the NBA, which can prove to be challenging for both mothers and fathers.

With increasing pressure on our young athletes to perform and excel, does participating in team sports give them the proper tools to be successful in the real world or does it unknowingly teach them how to form cliques that focus on excluding others? Watching my son attend basketball camp and play in tournaments and championships has shown me what a "big man on campus" can feel like. He fist pumps or chest bumps all the boys he knows. Little boys are in awe of him, and opponents are initially afraid of his size, but once they realize what a friendly kid he is, they exude admiration in their eyes. Since I have not had the opportunity to participate in organized sports, this is foreign territory to me. I never experienced this type of veneration at such a young age, and I find it remarkable to witness it as a mother and social-personality psychologist. These experiences show me how playing a team sport can be political and used as a way to gain entry into American culture. We are lucky that his skillset and height make him a desirable player, as numerous coaches have actively tried to recruit him for their teams, but we also see how other Asian kids who do not have the height or skills may be overlooked and ignored based on current stereotypes of Asian male athletes. How does being invisible and the last to be chosen affect their sense of belonging? These become opportunities to teach our children that not every individual has the same affinity for sports, and sometimes talent alone is not enough to become a part of this fraternity.

In many instances, our children are learning real-world strategies on how to get ahead, but at what cost? Hearing Donald Trump casually dismiss his derogatory comments about women as "locker room talk" worried me as a mother. I still hear comments from other parents who perpetuate notions of male privilege with their belief that "boys will be boys." I wonder if my son will be witness to these misogynist views when he is in the locker room. Throughout my children's lives, I have consistently told them that they may hear and see things from their peers that are unacceptable in our home, and witnessing these trespasses does not give them the right to engage in those activities. We also teach them that when they see injustices occurring, they must speak up and/or tell an adult. I feel these are critical conversations to have with our children because they do make a difference in shaping their belief systems. I have had numerous mothers, some I know and some I do not, tell me how my son stepped up and intervened when their child was being bullied. Those instances give me hope that maybe I am doing a decent job as a mother.

Being a part of a team does offer certain experiences for our children that will benefit them in the real world. Participating in team sports can foster alliances that often benefit men in the workplace. Sharing an affinity for a particular sports team, playing fantasy sports, or playing on a corporate team are all common ways for men to bond in the workplace and encourage networking (Shankar et al. 59). The problem lies when certain groups (e.g., women, LGBTQIA, people of colour, etc.) cannot share in the masculine camaraderie that is typical in corporate America. Therefore, how do mothers teach their sons to be mindful of this disparity? My answer lies in using each transgression as an opportunity to teach our sons and daughters that they are valuable individuals who matter and deserve respect and dignity. This is where our family values come into play: we instill in our children the values of honouring elders, filial piety, and self-respect. Even when the world seems cold and discriminatory, they know that they always have the support of their family to fall back on. In the movie, *Linsanity*, Yao stated how playing in the NBA was characterized by pressure—from playing in games, the media, and even fans. But one hope he shared with Lin was the value of spending time with those who provide unconditional support such as family. I can only hope that the love and support we instill in our children is enough to buffer them from a world still debating whether Asians should be accepted in the sports arena, which leads to specific mothering challenges I have to contend with as a Chinese mother.

My Personal Mothering Challenges

I still struggle with harnessing my anger when I hear racial epithets from opposing players and their parents. My son has been called Yao Ming; he's been told him to go back to China; and he's suffered other derogatory name-calling that targets him because he is Chinese. I find my anger is directed more toward the parents, and I believe that the mere fact that my son defies so many of the Asian male stereotypes makes him a target of their hostility because they do not know how to categorize him. He does not fit into the nerdy, socially awkward, and unathletic Asian male stereotype. He creates feelings of unease because he challenges these parents to redefine and rethink their definitions of Asian-ness and athleticism. Karen Pyke has described the robustness of these negative Asian male stereotypes because the process of acculturating and assimilating into U.S. culture encourages the denigration of nonwhite bodies while upholding white masculinity as the ideal (2). Combining this stereotypic thinking with an intense in-group and out-group mentality where we identify with our own team and denigrate the opposing team can result in an intense range of emotions. These feelings are not limited towards opposing teams, as I have also been the target of animosity for merely being his mother.

As a spectator, I have witnessed significant differences in how fathers and mothers are treated during these games. On multiple occasions, the opposing coach has come to me in an attempt to recruit my son for their team. I was always professional and took their unsolicited information, but in doing so, I noticed that I became the recipient of numerous dirty looks from our coach and the fathers on our team. It was striking because the mothers did not behave in such a manner. Perhaps the other mothers did not interpret the attempts to recruit my son as an indicator that my son's abilities overshadowed their sons, but many of the fathers interpreted this as a hostile act on my part. I never knew that the basketball court could be such fertile ground to examine gender differences, but it can teach us so much about the subtle and not so subtle assumptions of gendered power hierarchies. When I drive my son to games by myself, I always feel that I have to keep my guard up in dealing with the male coaches, but when I sit with a mom I am friendly with or my husband, there are less dirty looks, as if the group dynamic changed how I was being viewed. I may not have blatantly called out those men for their disrespectful behaviour, but my eye contact and stance showed them I was not going to tolerate any sexist behaviour. I question whether this behaviour is due to my being Chinese, which may have elicited their stereotypical beliefs of an Asian woman as demure, quiet, and passive.

Another challenge as a Chinese mother concerns the difficulties of convincing family members to understand the value we place on sports when we sometimes choose to attend our son's games over family functions. What these family members may not be aware of is how participating in competitive sports in Shanghai is viewed as a projection of regional and national pride that aims to unite communities through participation or spectatorship (Lozada 215). Living in the United States, sharing knowledge, spectatorship, and participation in team sports can be important entryways into American society (Shankar et al. 58). As a child, I recalled many happy times spent watching the World Wrestling Federation (now World Wrestling Entertainment) with my father and grandfather while eating Chinese peanuts that could only be purchased at Asian grocery stores. The simplicity of good versus evil being played out within the wrestling ring seemed to transcend the language barrier as my father and grandfather knew limited English, yet we all cheered for the good guys and jeered at the bad ones. We would comment on the idiosyncrasies of each wrestler and revel as they entertained us each evening. Sharing expert knowledge in American sports, even wrestling, can be especially helpful to those who are standing outside the margins, such as immigrants, women, persons of colour, or any individual who does not fit the white, heteronormative male model. For these individuals, participation in team sports or spectatorship becomes a useful tool to bypass marginalization (Shankar et al. 58).

In many instances, it is a constant juggling process to seamlessly incorporate both cultures in our home. We still participate in many Chinese holidays (e.g., Chinese New Year, Autumn Festival, Spring Festival, etc.), but we also make time in our busy schedules to support our son's love of basketball and attend his games. My husband, who played high school football, did not have that luxury. Being first-generation immigrants, his parents thought he was joining a gang when he told them he wanted to pursue his love of football and play on his high school football team. That mentality, however, was not uncommon at that time among new immigrants. Working long hours to merely survive was typical of first-generation immigrant parents, which resulted in their inability to offer financial and emotional support in terms of attending games, paying for camp, or showing an interest in football.

Working in corporate America, my husband can attest to how having played team sports can be an asset in the business world. His ability to participate in sports-related conversations and play collectively on corporate teams makes him privy to certain networks that are often inaccessible to colleagues who did not partake in sports. The ability to participate in these conversations is a vital tool that helps create a smooth transition from outsider to insider within American corporate culture (Shankar et al. 53). Unfortunately, there are family members who do not value these connections as we have been on the receiving end of family friction when they do not see the value of attending basketball games in lieu of family functions. Although we try to blend both cultures in our home by negotiating ways to help our son embrace athleticism, academics, and family, the friction we encounter makes me question whether it is due to the fact that my son challenges the traditional Asian male stereotypes, which can make others feel uncomfortable. My experiences of mothering my son have taught me that it is not my responsibility to assuage other people's discomfort.

Conclusion

The greatest lessons I have learned in writing this chapter is that mothering and sports can be political, and in encouraging my son to pursue his love of basketball, I am teaching a new generation of mothers and their young athletes to break barriers, to find their voices to rebel against injustices, and to constantly challenge the status quo. In researching this topic, attending games, interacting with other parents and their children, dealing with coaches, and speaking with my son, I have gained much insight on the meaning of basketball, which surpasses what happens on the court. For me, basketball serves as an important entryway into American culture and offers our young athletes multiple benefits, but not everyone is granted the same privileges. My observations as a Chinese basketball mom are merely one facet of how race and class affect youth basketball. My own experiences reveal important unspoken and often invisible factors influencing who gets afforded the privilege to participate in and reap the benefits of youth basketball and who does not gain access to these advantages. Fortunately, there are health initiatives as well as a growing field in health pedagogy diligently working to reduce these disparities and inequities for all children. In the end, I asked my son how he felt when kids called him Yao Ming. I know it made me angry because I interpreted such comments as blatantly racist and that they were making fun of him, which brought out the protective mama bear in me, but his reply struck me. He said that he didn't think it was a bad thing and explained to me that it was because Yao Ming was a great basketball player, tall like him, and the first Chinese player in the NBA to be inducted into the Basketball Hall of Fame. It made me pause for a moment and reexamine my own biases, as I could not let my own experiences of racism colour my children's experiences. They are living in a different time, and although I tend to see the darkness of certain people's words because I grew up during a time where there were no well-known Asian or Asian American basketball players, I also need to see basketball through my son's eyes. On one hand, it is an exciting time to be Chinese and involved in sports because we are witnessing groundbreaking realities. We are actively shattering stereotypes of Asian men and forging our own paths that were built upon the shoulders of numerous Asian and Asian American basketball players who used sports as a way to resist segregation and discrimination (Yep 7). When angry parents and opponents call my son Yao Ming, I am going to try to see it as something positive that should evoke pride because Yao and Lin are the beneficiaries of past Asian trailblazers, such as Willie Woo Wong, Helen Wong, and Wataru Misaka. These athletes are challenging Asian stereotypes so my son can stand on their shoulders and have a more inclusive experience in organized team sports. So the next time I hear these comments, rather than feel frustration and anger, I may just sit back, puff out my chest with pride, and say, "Yeah, he is my Yao Ming!", all the while being grateful that my son's experiences in basketball are teaching me new ways to mother the athlete in him.

Works Cited

Chua, Amy. *Battle Hymn of the Tiger Mother*. Penguin Publishing Group, 2011.

Dagkas, Symeon. "Problematizing Social Injustice in Health Pedagogy and Youth Sport: Intersectionality of Race, Ethnicity, and Class." *Research Quarterly for Exercise and Sport*, vol. 87, no. 3, 2016, pp. 221-29.

Farred, Grant. *Phantom Calls: Race and Globalization of the NBA*. Prickly Paradigm Press, 2006.

Grasmuck, Sherri. *Protecting Home: Class, Race, and Masculinity in Boys' Baseball*. Rutgers University Press, 2005.

Hauser, Christine. "Judge's Sentencing in Massachusetts Sexual Assault Case Reignites Debate on Privilege." The New York Times, 24 Aug. 2016, https://www.nytimes.com/2016/08/25/us/david-becker-massachusetts-sexual-assault.html. Accessed 23 June 2018.

"Jeremy Lin: Too Flagrant Not to Call." *YouTube*, uploaded by JAD 7534, 5 Apr. 2016, www.youtube.com/watch?v=KvaM0pMj-8o. Accessed 16 June 2018.

Lee, Bruce. "By Not Protecting Jeremy Lin, NBA Sends Wrong Messages to Children." *Forbes*, 17 Apr. 2016, http://www.forbes.com/sites/brucelee/2016/04/17/by-not-protecting jeremy-lin-nba-sends-wrong-messages-to-children/#635972f2729e. Accessed 31 October 2016.

Linsanity. Directed by Evan Jackson Leong, staring Jeremy Lin, Arowana Films, 2013.

Lozada, Eriberto. "Cosmopolitanism and Nationalism in Shanghai Sports." *City & Society*, vol. 18, no. 2, 2006, pp. 207-30.

Marsh, Herbert W., and Sabina Kleitman. "School Athletic Participation: Mostly Gain with Little Pain." *Journal of Sport & Exercise Psychology*, vol. 25, no. 2, 2003, pp. 205-28.

NBA Official. "NBA Response to New York Times Story on Flagrant Fouls and Charlotte Hornets Guard Jeremy Lin." *NBA*, 15 April, 2016, official.nba.com/nba-response-new-york-times-story-jeremy-lin/. Accessed 16 Aug. 2016.

NBA Video Rulebook. "Flagrant Foul, Penalty 1 (High Wrap Up around Neck)." *NBA*, videorulebook.nba.com/archive/flagrant-foul-penalty-1-high-wrap-up-around-neck/. Accessed 16 Aug. 2016.

Ong, Anthony D., et al. "Racial Microaggressions and Daily Well-Being Among Asian Americans." *Journal of Counseling Psychology*, vol. 60, no. 2, 2013, pp. 188-99.

Pyke, Karen. "Internalized Gendered Racism in Asian American Women?" Accounts of Asian and White Masculinities." Public Sociologies, American Sociological Association, 17 August 2004, Hilton San Francisco & Renaissance Parc 55 Hotel, San Francisco, CA. Conference Presentation.

Shankar, Shalini et al. "Reflections on Sport Spectatorship and Immigrant Life." Asian American Sporting Cultures, edited by Stanley I. Thangaraj et al., New York University Press, 2016, pp. 53-72.

Shakib, Sohaila, et al. "Athletics as a Source for Social Status Among Youth: Examining Variation by Gender, Race/Ethnicity, And Socioeconomic Status." Sociology of Sport Journal, vol. 28, no. 3, 2011, pp. 303-28.

Thangaraj, Stanley. Desi Hoop Dreams: Pickup Basketball and the Making of Asian American Masculinity. New York University Press, 2015.

The Aspen Institute. "Sport for All Play for Life: A Playbook to Get Every Kid in the Game." Sports & Society Program, 27 Jan. 2015, www. aspeninstitute.org/publications/sport-all-play-life-playbook-get-every-kid-game/. Accessed 5 January 2017.

Visek, Amanda J., et al. "The Fun Integration Theory: Toward Sustaining Children and Adolescents Sport Participation." Journal of Physical Activity & Health, vol. 12, no. 3, 2015, pp. 424-33.

Wu, Ellen. The Color of Success. Asian Americans and the Origins of the Model Minority. Princeton University Press, 2014.

Yep, Kathleen. Outside the Paint: When Basketball Ruled at the Chinese Playground. Temple University Press, 2009.

Chapter 4

Ecofeminism Meets the Team Mom: Eco-Momma as Cultural Change Broker

Pamela Morgan Redela

The following discussion will expand upon Michael Messner's work on gender in youth sports as well as Arlie Hochschild's analysis of "the second shift" in order to deepen their insights. Their feminist analysis reveals how the gender hierarchy works in youth sports and home life, respectively. Adding the ecofeminist layer allows us to look at the consumerist dimension of youth sports and offers a way out of the dualist "male equals superior and female equals inferior" thinking, which rules under heteropatriarchy. In my view, by rejecting this dualism, we can create a more enriching experience for all involved. This discussion also recognizes the level of privilege in the situation at hand. The phenomenon I am discussing is not exclusive to white communities, but it is definitely part of the economically privileged, suburban realm of those families who can afford the luxury of paid youth sports participation. Issues of race, gender, and class privilege are not lost on the author.

Introduction

I think I've always been a feminist. I cannot remember a time in my life when I did not notice, contemplate, or question what I now know as "the heteropatriarchal, sex-gender system," which rules our world. (I was five years old when I first told a boy "you've got two hands, the food's in the fridge!" when he commanded "where's my breakfast?" in the kindergarten play kitchen.) When it came to sports, I could always compete with the boys in neighbourhood baseball and football, but growing up in the 1970s, opportunities for organized team sports were limited by access and by my family's limited economic means. As the 1980s rolled around, girls' high school sports were growing, but my slight build didn't give me the edge I needed to make the team. Although I continue to this day to be physically active, the experiences with sports and sexism in my youth instilled a desire to be a "change maker" as an adult.

I am now a mother, and since having children, I have become much more focused on and concerned with environmental issues. This combination of my feminism, my intensive style of motherhood, and my interest in environmentalism has led me to ecofeminism. That makes me an eco-momma! Who is an eco-momma, and why is she of any interest? An eco-momma is one of a community of mothers whose parenting focuses on environmentalism and has little use of patriarchal hierarchy in her lifestyle. Dad changes as many diapers and does as much laundry and dishes as mom, and mom and dad become a united front—rather than dad acting as disciplinarian and mom acting as nurturer—when enforcing household rules. What does an eco-momma do? Whether she works outside the home or not, she does her best to buck the consumer-capitalist lifestyle by adhering to the "reduce, reuse, recycle" mantra in her daily life by seeking out environmentally friendly products, recycling, shopping at second-hand stores for clothing and other household merchandise, supporting local businesses and organic farming practices, and raising her children to do the same. Although dad is an active part of household maintenance and childcare, the eco-momma also uses an attachment style of mothering in her household, which is often characterized in the negative as "helicopter parenting." But from an ecofeminist perspective, this dependence on mother can be transformative. When the mother has a true seat of power in the household, her nurturing prowess can represent a rejection of a hypermasculine culture focused on winning and privileging reason over emotion. This is very different from the "controlling mother" stereotype, since the father does a fair amount of nurturing himself; all members of the home, regardless of gender, hold a feminine style of nurturing in high regard. As such, this stance involves a rejection of classic liberal feminism, which encourages women and girls to become "one of the boys" in sports and business, yet still remain "sexy" in the heteropatriarchal sense of the word. The eco-momma celebrates her feminine power and uses it to rebel against the capitalist hetero-patriarchy, not to serve it.

Gender Dynamics and the Degradation of the Feminine

As the mother of two athletic children, I find myself continuously involved in their sports team activities. My community-minded inclina-tions, largely drawn from ecofeminist principles—such as reclaiming the right to care for each other and our homes (Plant)—often put me in the volunteer position of "team mom." Who is the team mom? She is sometimes the wife of the coach, but she is always the mother of a child on the team. (My kids have only been on two teams headed by a female coach in over ten years of dedicated, year-round sports involvement.)

The work of team mom is highly gendered, heteronormative, and consumer oriented. Men are coaches, a high-prestige position, and women are helpers in low-prestige positions, reflecting the overarching heteropatriarchal norms of the world around us. Coach work equals quality learning time for the kids. Team mom work equals motherwork: providing snacks, bandages, trophies, coach gifts, volunteer support for league fundraising events, and team party planning. This carework goes without compensation, as do most coaching duties, but in the competitive youth sports arena, coaches are paid. In that realm, team managers carrying a much more substantial workload in terms of paperwork and financial planning are not paid, and in five years of involvement in this area of youth sport, I have only seen one male in the position, and his wife carried a substantial portion of the workload. Both of my children's female-headed teams had a team mom instead of a team dad. In these ten years of volunteer involvement, I have had only one team dad experience, which was refreshing, but nowhere near the norm.

Michael Messner's book *It's All for the Kids: Gender, Families, and Youth Sports* offers a sociological analysis, with a feminist bent, of gender dynamics in youth sports. The book presents multiple examples of the sexism I describe above as it appears in youth sports, ranging from coaching comments we've all heard like "You throw like a girl!", to discrimination against women in leadership (One chapter is titled: "We don't like chick coaches."). In the area of volunteering, comments like "Snacks and team party? We'll leave that to the moms!" are common in my experience, and this is echoed in Messner's work. His chapter "'Looking for a Team Mom': Separating the Men from the Moms" spoke to my soul! His interviews with parents of young kids participating in baseball and soccer leagues in suburban Southern California (my very economically privileged and majority white neck of the woods) reveal a common thread: nobody wants to be the team mom, and almost everyone (women included) disregards and degrades any work marked as feminine.

For example, Messner offers the following fieldnotes from an eleven- and twelve-year-old boys' Little League team practice: "In addition to myself, three more dads have volunteered to assist Coach Dean... I overhear one assistant coach say to Dean, 'So, are the women still laying low?' Dean, with a chuckle, replies, 'Yes! So far no team mom!' The assistant coach quips, "I guess nobody wants to do it, huh?" (Messner 24). The situation continues for a week as Coach Dean continues to look for a team mom. Messner concludes as follows:

> I'm standing alone by the dugout, and behind me sitting in the stands are three moms. One of them says, in hushed tones, "I hear they are still looking for a team mom." Another giggles and whispers conspiratorially, "I'm laying low on that one." Another laughs and says, more loudly, "Me too. I'm sure they can find a dad to do it." They all laugh ... By the second game, the "team mom" is Tina, Coach Dean's wife. (Messner 25)

I've lived this same scenario every single season, of every single sport my kids play. As a feminist, it is surely frustrating to see the sexist gender dynamics in these types of situations, and so far, it seems that many others see the inequality and injustice too, but not many are willing to do anything about it. The end result of this scenario in Messner's study, and in my own experience, is that absent a willing volunteer, the coach's wife ends up covering the team mom duties.

From this example, we can see that the tenets of liberal feminism have definitely reached the masses. People generally agree that a woman can do anything a man can do, but the analysis stops there. The overarching sentiment is that what men do is better than what women do, so everyone, women included, should strive to be male. This type of thinking results in most everyone seeing carework as menial and invaluable; the stuff someone "gets stuck with" rather than vital daily activity that makes life happen. If the so-called woman's work of food preparation, cleaning, laundry, and schedule keeping doesn't happen, no one is well enough, clean enough, or organized enough to go to work or school, or do sports.

The overvaluation of all things male is the prime culprit in this scenario, and this is where the eco-momma shows up in her unabashedly feminine way to remind everyone that selling out to the capitalist heteropatriarchy is not all it's cracked up to be. She makes no excuses for her nurturing way of being (providing positive feedback and cheering from the stands, and making sure all of the kids are hydrated!), and she calls on both moms and dads for volunteer work over the season. Most dads say they are "too busy with work" to help out at the bake sale, but their working wives find the time to pick up something to donate. When the volunteer request involves setting up the fundraiser (carrying tables and supplies for the bake sale), that's when dads will step up. Gendered work patterns are hard to break. From personal experience, I can add that after persistent prodding, each season I do get more and more participation from those men who have flexible work schedules, which is heartening.

An important investigation into the devaluation of motherwork is Arlie Hochschild's research on "the second shift." Her groundbreaking work from the 1980s revealed that in two-income households, the responsibility of childcare and housework that was dumped on women amounted to an extra month of twenty-four-hour workdays. The families she interviewed included a range of household dynamics: men who refused to do anything child or home related to men who participated in home life, but at their convenience. These dynamics continue to be a source of contention in the new millennium, but things are definitely improving since Hochschild and the feminist movement put the topic on the table. In my own experience, I have seen many positive changes in who is doing the parenting and household maintenance; the expectations on men's participation in family life are steadily increasing. What hasn't changed, however, is the idea that childcare and housework—motherwork—are feminine tasks and are still regarded as negative. The following summation from Hochschild still resonates in 2018: "Sadly enough, women are more often the lightning rods for family aggressions aroused by the speed-up of work and family life. They are the 'villains' in a process of which they are also the primary victims. More than the longer hours, the sleeplessness, and feeling torn, this is the saddest cost to women of the extra month a year" (262). When it comes to matters of chores and daily tasks, most mothers are still regarded as "nags" to be reviled, whereas most fathers are "disciplinarians" to be respected. Cooking, cleaning, and childcare are still thought to be menial tasks, whereas car repair and yard work are productive activities, which deserve praise and recognition when completed. The feminine-masculine, low-prestige-high-prestige dichotomy is hard to miss here. A frustrating part of this issue is that when men perform feminine work, they are praised for it, whereas women are expected to do these tasks and are only recognized (and in the negative) when they are not doing the work.

This cultural degradation of all things feminine is where the eco-momma comes in. We all know that without motherwork, life does not happen. If we have no food to eat, we don't survive. If we have no clean clothes, we may face social difficulties at school, work, etc. If we leave children uneducated in social niceties, we may eventually lose civil society. Despite these details, the culture still regards motherwork as "menial," as something no one, women included, wants to do. As such, those who do the work see themselves as "getting stuck with it" and, in turn, those performing undervalued work are often regarded as unlucky and undesirable. This dynamic becomes more clear when we look at class dynamics and when we look at who the nannies and housekeepers are and how much they are paid; in Southern California, financially able households (mostly white) hire out the motherwork to low-income women (mostly Latina). Regardless of her economic status and whether she works outside the home or not, the eco-momma does not hire out the housekeeping and childcare; she demands that the family unit participate in this endeavour in an effort to strengthen the family bond and to reject the degradation of so-called woman's work as something to be hired out to a woman of lower status, both economically and socially. To her, even though this arrangement sometimes results in the house being a bit messy and dusty until family cleaning hour on the weekend and in the kids having to spend some time doing unstructured play at home while she and dad catch up on work emails (the horror! children forced to be creative with their free time!), it is better than propagating heteropatriarchal, racist, and classist world order.

From here, we can see that the sports team is in many ways a microcosm of the traditional heteropatriarchal household. The coach is the father, who has the high-prestige position of leader and disciplinarian, whereas team mom is the mother, who takes care of the little things and carries out the father's edicts.

Ecofeminism to the Rescue!

Ecofeminism makes connections between the oppression and exploitation of women in patriarchal societies and the exploitation of the earth. Societies that view the earth as a resource to be used also view women in a similar light. For example, in the U.S., the earth's resources have been historically viewed as in need of technological use or manipulation in order to reach their maximum use value. In this same culture, women's bodies have a similar use value; women are used as sex objects, as childrearers, housekeepers, and cooks. A woman as a career-oriented human being is a recent formulation in U.S. culture, and as such, a woman as an individual is not something the culture is openly embracing. The word "woman" still carries with it an image of mom with baby on hip, toddler in tow, and broom in hand.

Given this cultural background, women's taking on the role of caregiver in youth sports is seen as natural. Collecting money from parents for gifts, trophies, and end of season parties, along with managing after-game snack schedules, is work that coaches are not expected to perform. Let's let one of the moms handle that! The eco-momma resists and disrupts the status quo, even in its embrace of characteristics that the culture labels "feminine," such as emotional sensitivity, a focus on the wellbeing of children, and expertise in multitasking. In my view, this disruption is needed, and in my experience, the majority of parents surprisingly welcome it. Ecofeminist scholar Ynestra King argues the following:

Ecofeminism suggests ... a recognition that although the nature-culture dualism is a product of culture, *we can nonetheless consciously choose* not to sever the woman-nature connection by joining male culture. Rather, we can use it as a vantage point for creating a different kind of culture and politics that would integrate intuitive, spiritual, and rational forms of knowledge, embracing both science and magic insofar as they enable us to transform the nature-culture distinction and to envision and create a free, ecological society. (my emphasis, 23)

What ecofeminism has taught me is that the misogyny of hetero-patriarchy has degraded the feminine so much that even women have rejected it, as the above examples attest. Team mom is a hyperfeminized role. The duties are related to housework and mothering, which no one who has embraced heteropatriarchal norms wants to do. Why have we come to regard the activities essential for our survival as well as those that simply make survival easier as something to be loathed and seen as having little economic and social value?

As I previously stated, the overvaluation of all things masculine in our world is a main source of this issue. Although I certainly love feminism, the liberal "superwoman" feminism of the 1970s and 1980s did none of us any long-term favours. Yes, it is wonderful that women gained access to the workforce and higher education in much larger numbers, but we did so without getting any relief on the home front. Housework and childcare were then—and to a certain degree are still now—thought of as women's primary responsibility. Men help out, but they are not held socially responsible when the house is a dusty wreck when guests arrive or when children are unruly in public. In the new millennium, men are stepping up in much larger numbers and in more substance in the home realm, which is wonderful. It is going to take persistence and social change, in the form of men pressuring other men, to keep up the momentum.

The Nitty-Gritty of "Eco-Momma Meets Team Mom"

Ecofeminism engages with and reevaluates the feminine role in order to restore balance to society. A closer look at the example of team mom allows us to explore the ways that environmentally conscious feminism can change the way people think about gendered work. On average, the duties of team mom are as follows:

- Collect player roster from the coach to make or order a team banner. Some leagues use a printing service for these banners; others (mostly in younger age levels of soccer and softball) push for homemade. This work nearly always falls to the team mom, and it can be extensive when the homemade version is required. There is no out-of-pocket expense for families if the team can find a sponsor. This sponsor will usually be a local business or a business belonging to a parent from the team, or a business in which a parent of a team member is employed. If no sponsor is found, the team must scrape together as much as $500.

- Gather contact information for team, and set up and run a team website. There are great free services that have popped up for this, such as Shutterfly, TeamStuff, and TeamSnap. All require about two hours of work to set up plus weekly check-ins for scheduling of practices, games, and any other team communications.
- Collect money from parents to cover costs of a fundraising item for the league, a coach gift for the end of the season, trophies for the kids, and supplies for an end of season party. These expenses can run anywhere from $20 to $50 a family on top of the over $200 of league fees required to join a team. (At the club level of play, fees range from $1400 to $3000 per season.)
- Make sure all players have proper paperwork for team picture day.
- Coordinate pickup and distribution of uniforms and pictures.
- Coordinate volunteers from among team families for league fundraising events. (And if no one volunteers, she does the work herself.)
- Coordinate any team social events, such as the end of season awards ceremony. This includes ordering of trophies and medals for the players.

To be successful in this work, the team mom has to put in some work on the frontend with finding a team sponsor, locating a banner, and starting the website. The mid-season part is a matter of communicating with parents in person before, during, and after games. The backend work of buying the coach a gift and planning a team party can be as labour intensive or relaxed as one wants to make it. This is certainly a task that precludes women who have demanding work schedules. Most of the women I interact with who take on this role are either stay-at-home moms or work part-time jobs. Those of us who take this on while doing full-time work are in fields with more flexible schedules like sales and teaching. (The reasons for the feminization of part-time and flexible work schedules become clear with this type of example; the system needs women just available enough to both contribute to the economy and do the carework, and just financially dependent enough to maintain the heteropatriarchal ideal of the nuclear family.)

An interesting aspect of this social phenomenon is the gendering of this work, which results in its devaluation. Messner notes the following:

Despite the importance of the work that team parents are doing, it is not often recognized as anywhere equivalent to the importance of the work done by coaches. Of course, the team parent typically puts in fewer hours of labor than does the head coach.... Yet the team parent's work remains largely invisible, and, as we have seen, coaches sometimes talk about team parents' contributions as trivial or unimportant. Several coaches, when asked about the team parent job, kind of pooh-poohed it as "not very hard to do," or "an easy job." (Messner 45)

As a team mom, I can agree that the work is easy and not very hard to do if one has good organization and time-management skills. As a feminist, I am drawn to problematize the heteropatriarchal logic that equates "easy to do" to "below my paygrade, and therefore low-status 'women's work.'" The sexism in gendered work patterns that permeates youth sports (and many other realms of daily life) is challenged by eco-momma in her insistence on placing value on "motherwork" by actively involving other parents (men included) in "Team Mom" duties and refusing to tolerate sexist comments in the stands. (Whenever I hear "You throw like a girl!" or anything similar at a game, I yell out "no sexism on the field!" from the stands, and I've happily heard some men doing the same.) Messner's analysis does a great job of pointing out where this injustice lies, and he offers a few examples of resistance—such as the persistence of some female coaches to prove themselves in all male spaces, and the work of some team moms to make sure all duties are divided evenly among the families (Messner 36). The next step is the insistence on male participation in and appreciation of a decidedly feminine style of daily carework.

To offer a specific example, there was one season of Little League baseball that pushed me into bringing the eco-momma into the team mom role. Our coach was a very traditional male. As head coach, he was definitely the man in charge. He had four assistant coaches who ran practices. He laid out the plan, directed the assistant coaches and kids, and watched with clipboard and pencil in hand and took copious notes. Come game day, he would do more of the same: he would put together the lineup and field-position plans for each inning and then he would run the game from the dugout.

His wife took on team mom duties, and we had an expensive and a labour-intensive season. Each family was asked to contribute $100 to cover trophies and a coach gift. Additional expenses were required for snacks and team parties. Each week's snack was to be fruit for the dugout (sliced oranges or watermelon) and an after-game drink and treat, which most of the time was juice boxes and potato chips, or granola bars. (Nothing gets an eco-momma riled up more than sugar-laden treats marketed as health food. Quaker brand chocolate chip granola bar, anyone?) Some parents try for healthier options such as water bottles and fruit skewers, but most people rush in with their store-bought option at the last minute, whereas others distribute prepurchased tickets to the snack bar because they forgot it was their week. All options run each family about $25 to $30, and all involve some sort of sugary junk-food snack in a landfill-bound container or wrapping. The kicker here is that the majority of game times fall just before lunch or dinner.

There were two team parties that season: one at the beginning of the season and one at the end. Both parties involved each family signing up to bring items from a prepared list, such as hot dogs, burgers, chips, fruit salad, drinks, cups, and plates. This was about another $15 to $20 per family for each party. That puts us at between $150 and $200 over and above the $200 league fees. This can be very difficult for families with limited economic means.

All of this may seem normal or even the fun part of youth sport activity, but as an eco-momma, all I could see was the amount of sugar and waste going into the snack and party rituals. This is one of the most disturbing parts of youth sports. Most sports facilities have a snack bar of some sort filled not only with junk food but also with lots of "junk" to go along with that "food"—Styrofoam cups, bowls, and plates as well as disposable utensils. More and more facilities are providing recycling containers for the soda cans and Gatorade bottles, but there are still a lot of nonrecyclable and noncompostable items used, which is frustrating for the environmentally conscious. Combine this with the one-time use of such products as the vinyl banners and trophies, which end up in a box in the attic or the landfill, and we've got an environmentalist's nightmare on our hands.

Conclusion: This Is What Resistance Looks Like

When I realized that most parents and kids can understand the disparities and damages that the sexist binary creates, I decided it was an appropriate time to introduce eco-momma to the team. I ended up introducing her to the elementary school and the university too, but we'll keep things focused on one area for now.

When my partner decided to take on head coach duties, I took on team mom duties without hesitation. I was able to get a friend from the team to make the role "co-team parent," and we made a few ecofeminist-friendly changes to the way things were done. First, we did away with the after-game snack. We were nervous about this one, but to our pleasure, we were met with cheers of joy by all parents. As it turned out, lots of other families felt the same as I did about filling their kids up with a sugary snack before lunch or dinner. They also resented the headache and expense of this task. Below are other changes we made:

- No disposable water bottles in the dugout. We brought a large dispenser cooler filled with ice water for the kids to use to refill their reusable water bottles. Seeing no huge bags of recycle waste after every game made this eco-momma very happy.

- No coach gift or individual trophies at the end of the season. Instead, each family contributed a total of $20 for the season, which covered a generous donation to the league (at coach's request) to cover supplies and contribute to a scholarship fund, with enough left over for an end of the season pizza party. In lieu of a trophy, we took action shots of the kids throughout the season, and coach gave each player a signed, framed copy of their best photo.

- No lists were made, and no duties assigned for the end of season party. The end of season party was a potluck for grown up dishes, and truly pot "luck" style: and we didn't end up with fifteen bags of chips! There were lots of creative salads, vegetable plates and fruit kabobs to enjoy along with the pizza.

Overall, we had a much more relaxed season on the parent side of things, and ended up with many of the same parents and routine for the next season. I was very happy with the results of the experiment, and experienced very little friction from parents. In the two seasons I did this, there were, however, two instances of resistance. A grandmother of a player brought cupcakes or cookies to every game she attended, even when asked not to. This was surely disappointing, but the parents took it in stride, since she only came to the weekend games, and the ecofeminist in me secretly enjoyed her persistence in proudly proclaiming the role of Grandma. The second instance was a parent who objected to a lack of trophies at the end of the season. Luckily, the parent was pleasantly surprised by and approved of the action shot memento.

These changes in the team mom activities may not seem like much in the larger picture but to eco-momma, incremental change is a principal part of her practice. In her article titled "Women and the Environment: Applying Ecofeminism to Environmentally-Related Consumption," Susan Dobscha offers the following:

Feminist research into our connection with the environment would look much different. It would place passion and emotion at the center of the research and focus on the connectedness that drives consumers to perform environmentally-related behaviors. The rational style of decision making is inadequate for explaining ERC. For example, what inspires a consumer to purchase recycled computer paper when it is a lesser quality product priced higher? Utility maximization theory fails to explain fully the highly context-dependent and emotionally-driven behaviors of the environmentally-conscious consumer ... Feminist research would instead locate the female consumer and her everyday experiences at the center of the research to determine whether passion and emotion are part of the process. (36)

These words truly sum up eco-momma's intervention and goals. In conclusion, this chapter has discussed how an eco-momma found success and solidarity in surprising ways when she rebelled against the consumer-capitalist model of motherhood. By making mindful shopping choices and combating heteropatriarchal standards and running an egalitarian, feminist-minded household, eco-momma can, by incremental means, help shift the paradigm of youth sports to be less dualistic, which allows us to revision "mothering" and "fathering" into a more gender fluid "parenting" that honors rather than degrades the feminine. Taking those values out of the home and into the public sphere of youth sports is a form of community intervention meant to influence the future toward a greener and less hierarchical place. What could be better than that?

Works Cited

Dobscha, Susan. "Women and the Environment: Applying Ecofeminism to Environmentally-Related Consumption." *Advances in Consumer Research*, vol. 20, 1993, pp. 36-40.

Hochschild, Arlie. *The Second Shift.* Penguin Books, 1989.

King, Ynestra. "The Ecology of Feminism and the Feminism of Ecology." *Healing the Wounds: The Promise of Ecofeminism*, edited by Judith Plant, New Society Publishers, 1989, pp. 18-28.

Messner, Michael A. *It's All for the Kids: Gender, Families, and Youth Sports.* University of California Press, 2009.

Plant, Judith, editor. *Healing the Wounds: The Promise of Ecofeminism.* New Society Publishers, 1989.

Chapter 5

Concussions in Sport and Girls in Women's Rugby: Effectively Resisting and Moving beyond Confining Gender Norms and Mother-Blame:

A Critical Discourse Analysis of the Rowan Stringer Case

Rebecca Jaremko Bromwich

"Sport has the power to change the world. It has the power
to inspire, the power to unite people that little else does."
—Nelson Mandela (qtd. in Carling 2)

In 2013, Rowan Stringer had every prospect for a bright future. She was a high-achieving, middle-class, seventeen-year-old in her senior year of high school, only weeks from graduation. She lived in the pleasant, middle-class Barrhaven suburb of Ottawa, Ontario—the clean, prosperous, and peaceful capital of Canada—with her parents, Kathleen and Gordon Stringer, and sister Cassie. She was captain of her high school girls rugby team, and was about to follow in her mother's footsteps, having been accepted to start nursing school at the University of Ottawa that fall. Her mother is a nurse at the Children's Hospital of Eastern Ontario (Obituary of Rowan Stringer).

However, tragically, in May 2013, on Mother's Day, Rowan Stringer died after succumbing to injuries incurred while playing women's rugby for the John McCrae Secondary School team. She died from a multiple head traumas while she was still suffering the effects of a first concussion—also received while playing a rugby game. The first hit occurred on Friday 3 May 2013 during a high school rugby tournament. She was removed from play after the incident but was allowed to return to play 6 May, the following Monday. During that game, she was hit in the head again, but she was not removed from play. Her symptoms returned, but she did not tell anyone. Two days later, on 8 May, she played another game. This one was her last. She was tackled, lost consciousness, and she never recovered. A coroner's inquest into Rowan's death found that she had actively concealed her injuries to continue playing, and it made forty-nine recommendations for improved concussion awareness and better treatment (Inquest decision).

Stringer's death has had a huge impact on her community, and has caused an outpouring of grief. The rugby pitch at Ken Ross Park, where Rowan Stringer once played, also officially became "Rowan's Pitch" in 2016 (Johnstone). In addition to community memorialization of Stringer's life, the grief over her death also transformed quickly into advocacy and law reform. As a result of the inquest and advocacy by her mother and a local MPP, among others, on 8 June 2016, a legislative proposal—a bill called Rowan's Law Bill 149, Rowan's Law Advisory Committee Act, 2016—was passed into law in Ontario. The resulting statute provides new guidance and legal protections for young athletes when concussions are suspected. It includes an expert advisory committee that will develop a plan and report to Ontario's premier in 2017 with recommendations for how to implement the recomm-endations of the coroner made in relation to the inquest into Stringer's death. Whereas the United States has many such laws, the statute is the first of its kind in Canada.

In this chapter, I present a critical discourse analysis of the public conversation and legal proceedings that together formed the public case in relation to the death of Rowan Stringer. The intersection of discourses surrounding the mother and girl in public documents produced in relation to Stringer's death and the inquest itself are critically analyzed. The study focuses on figures of the mother presented in these texts and specifically asks whether, and in what ways, the discursive frame of "mother-blame" is reproduced, reinscribed, and resisted in the public discourse surrounding her death. The analysis reveals that, overwhelmingly, discourses of mother-blame are actively resisted in the case. Consequently, Stringer's case is an inspiring instance of how a society and community can grapple with gender, mother-blame, and sport injuries in the wake of tragedy. The chapter situates this individual death and inquest in larger social trends and gendering processes involved with sport generally, women's sports specifically, and rugby in particular. I argue that the Stringer case demonstrates how participation by girls in nontraditional women's sports can afford a space for challenging traditional femininities, masculinities, misogynies, and discourses of mother-blame.

The Legal Case: Inquest and Law Reform

The Inquest

An inquest is a sociolegal inquiry using legal processes to ascertain a medical cause of death; it is presided over by a coroner, and a ruling as to cause of death, usually accompanied by recommendations, are made by a jury composed of five members of the community. Inquests are longstanding sociolegal practices, and have, since the eleventh century under the UK common law, been employed as a means to determine the cause, time, and mechanism of death (Wood). Inquest juries are tasked with determining answers to the following five questions:

- Who is deceased?
- Where did the death take place?
- When did the death occur?
- How did the death transpire (i.e., the medical cause)?
- By what means did the death happen (i.e., natural causes, accident, homicide, suicide, or is the cause of death undetermined)?

Although historically blame could be assigned by inquest juries, this is no longer within the inquest jury's duty or powers. Under Canada's constitutional division of powers, inquests are in provincial-territorial jurisdiction. In Ontario, where Rowan Stringer's inquest took place, inquest proceedings are governed by the Coroner's Act R.S.O. 1990, c-C.37. Inquest verdicts are unusual among legal documents because they are forward looking. They primarily make recommendations for future action instead of narratives of the past.

The Rowan Stringer inquest verdict was rendered on 3 June 2015. The cause of death was ruled to be an accident. Forty-nine recommendations were made by the presiding coroner, which is the procedure regularly followed in Ontario inquests. The first stated as follows:

> That the Government of Ontario adopt an Act ("Rowan's Law") governing all youth sport, both school-based and non-school based, which establishes the International Concussion Consensus Guidelines (Zurich) on Management of Concussion in Sports as the standard of practice for concussion management. The Act should recognize the importance of four criteria in protecting children and youth:
> • providing education on sport-related concussions to athletes, coaches and parents;
> • removing a child or youth athlete from play if a concussion is suspected;
> • ensuring the child or youth does not return to play until he or she has received medical clearance; and
> • ensuring appropriate return to learn and return to play strategies are in place (Inquest decision)

Law Reform

In a highly unusual instance of cooperation between all of Ontario's elected politicians, Rowan's Law passed 30 May 2016 to the Ontario Standing Committee on Justice by unanimous agreement of all three political parties. With the passage of this bill, Ontario became Canada's first jurisdiction to have concussion legislation. The legislation creates guidelines to ensure a minor playing sports is removed from the game if it is suspected he or she has suffered a concussion.

Rugby

Masculinity, Violence, and Community

Sociologists studying sports have unpacked how as forms of cultural practice and performance they are spaces in which social values and hierarchies are reproduced (Coakley). In general, sports have been linked to the maintenance and reinscription of male hegemonic power and patriarchal forms of social organization (Bryson; Hall, *Feminism and Sporting Bodies*). Sports have long been critiqued as a problematic venue of male-dominated discourses and practices. Yet women's sports are fast growing, and female athleticism provides new possibilities for understandings of and action by women and girls. Feminist criticism highlights both the problematic nature and potential of sports.

It has been several decades since Ann Hall suggested, "sport plays a significant role in the reproduction of a specifically patriarchal social order and could, therefore, be significant in the transformation of that order. At the very least, it can provide a site of resistance." ("Knowledge and Gender" 38) Although sports are a field in which widely assumed binary discourses of dominant males and subjugated females have been reinscribed, they can also be a space, especially where women participate in sports, to challenge those discourses. That challenge is threatened, though, when a girl or woman is hurt playing sport because the injury threatens to reinforce assumptions about girls' and women's fragility.

Certain sports are more linked to more gendering practices in the reconstruction and maintenance of masculinities or femininities. Rugby is most definitely one of these. It has been characterized as a space where its players are socialized into the larger social game of masculine gender. This game stereotypically involves performances of power, strength, and aggression as demonstrations of dominance and maleness. Rugby has even been characterized critically not just as a performance of masculinity but of misogyny (Pringle; Schacht).

Rugby has often been a space where sport is deployed to do the social work of "turning boys into men" (Light and Kirk). Rugby has been critiqued from a gender perspective as epitomizing performances of violent masculinity as valorized in sport. As Richard Light and David Kirk contend, rugby training is also training for "embodiment of a traditional, hegemonic form of masculinity" (163). Rugby is a rough contact sport that frequently produces injuries in its players. It is a game that many understand to be "the quintessential male sport" (O'Hanley 1), providing a space for enactment of "hyper-masculinity" (Light and Kirk 171).

However, gender is not the only larger social game being enacted on the rugby pitch. As was demonstrated in John Carlin's book *Playing the Enemy: Nelson Mandela and the Game That Made a Nation*, newly elected

President Nelson Mandela used rugby as a means to unite the races in postapartheid South Africa. Rugby has been generally analyzed as a game that can unify players and spectators, too, though around community through themes of "bodily discipline and the production of force" (Light and Kirk). Black and white players became a team and a nation rallied around them. And through this process, the stigmatized racial differences and horrific history between them was submerged and, to a certain extent, healed by their mutual representation as athletes.

Women's Rugby

Traditionally male dominated, rugby is becoming more popular as a sport for girls and women. Women's rugby is reported to be "Canada's fastest growing sport" (O'Hanley). Historians have begun to note how women have played rugby publicly, and even secretly, since the game became popular in the nineteenth century. However, until the 1970s, formal women's rugby teams were not part of Canadian university athletic programs. In the 1990s, the sport of women's rugby began to enjoy more widespread popularity (O'Hanley). Women's rugby is essentially the same as the game played by men. Whether played by women or men, rugby is a game played with the same rules, same field, and same equipment.

Although rugby has been criticized as a site for the production of violent masculinities, rugby in general and women's rugby in particular have also been analyzed as spaces where these ideologies can be challenged (Scrogum). Just as rugby presented a space for building community and challenging racism in postapartheid South Africa, it also presents girls and women who play with opportunities for camaraderie, community, and empowerment. They can be understood and represented as an athlete in ways that transcend gender. Women's rugby has potential as a "site for disruption of gender logic" (Scrogum 6).

The Study

This study involved a critical discourse analysis of public documents produced in the Rowan Stringer case. Texts were analyzed for the discursive figures of Rowan Stringer and her mother presented in them. To undertake this analysis, I looked critically at how the texts constructed gender, motherhood, and sports. I was specifically looking for the presence or absence of the phenomenon of mother-blame.

Feminist criticism has unpacked how cultural expectations of what constitutes "good motherhood" are very narrow and exclusionary (Caplan). Far from becoming a freer space in the contemporary moment than in the past, the identity and work of motherhood are social locations in which mothers are more than ever before judged, demonized, and stigmatized for issues and problems in their children's lives.

The phenomenon of mother-blame is pervasive in our late modern societies. As Paula Caplan writes, "blaming of mothers for virtually anything that goes wrong with their young or adult offspring, as well as for a host of societal ills such as juvenile delinquency and teenage pregnancy, has been described as similar to air pollution: it is pervasive but unnoticeable until one's attention is drawn to it or the environment changes" (2010). As Vanessa Reimer and Sarah Sahagian have further explored in their book *The Mother-Blame Game*, when something goes wrong in the lives of children and teenagers, it is very often the child's mother who is blamed for it.

Mothers are often blamed and shamed in a wide variety of ways for perceived deficiencies in their maternal practices. They also, though, actively resist ideologies of mother-blame by engaging in feminist mothering practices and by publicly challenging patriarchal discourses of "good motherhood." Encouraging children to stretch beyond traditional gender roles—such as signing one's daughter up to play sports, especially rough sports, like rugby—is one form of feminist mothering practice.

Documents studied in this research were produced in two discursive sites: media texts and official legal documents, such as the inquest decision, political speeches, and Hansard (parliamentary debate transcripts). As opposed to treating the inquest decision as the authoritative text for study as would be done in traditional doctrinal legal research, I inquire more broadly into the "public case" of Stringer's death. The case studied for the purposes of this research is defined as public documents produced in relation to the death of Rowan Stringer from 2013 until the passage of Rowan's Law in June 2016.

In this study, I critically unpack dominant discourses about girls, mothers, and sports in legal, media and expert sites, and how the discourses deployed in a variety of sites produced empowerment for the possibilities of girls' and women's subjectivities. This study attempts to understand socially produced meanings of girls, mothers, and athletes. It takes Rowan Stringer's case as a particular "event," in which confluences and tensions between ideologies and assumptions become visible (Johnson).

This study enquires into what Lauren Berlant calls the "caseness" of Rowan Stringer. The analysis involved asking how Stringer is constructed as a case. Of what broader social category is she held up to be an example? I work with the concept of figuration (De Laurentis)—a process by which a representation is given a particular form: "a figure is the simultaneously material and semiotic product of certain [discursive] processes" (Casteneda 3-4). A figuration is "a specific configuration of knowledges, practices and power" (Casteneda 3-4). Accordingly, I qualitatively study texts from media sources and official legal texts to determine what figurations of Rowan Stringer emerge in these cultural domains.

Critical discourse analysis (CDA) is a methodological framework for conducting research into how discourses function as instruments of power and control. It looks at social structures and processes involved in text production. It is an analytical way to make visible relationships of causality that are otherwise opaque and to see links between texts and broader social and cultural power relations and discursive processes.

The study analyzes how Stringer is represented and emerges as a figure in a variety of texts. More specifically, in this research, I looked at available news reports in print and online media about the Stringer inquest. I did so using a database search of the electronic journalism database called Factiva, looking for articles mentioning Rowan Stringer. This search yielded 436 articles. I also conducted searches using Google's media database. I additionally looked at the text of the inquest decision and the legal debates about Rowan's Law. I scrutinized the texts for figures of the mother the girl, and the athlete presented in them. I also looked for attributions of fault for Rowan's death.

Findings

Two key findings emerge from this critical discourse analysis. First, in media as well as formal legal texts, Stringer is overwhelmingly characterized as a "case" or a type "athlete," which is not significantly gendered. Stringer's death has been situated as a "case" of athletic injury in a manner that transcends and disrupts discourses of gender.

Second, her mother is never blamed for her death, and the texts overwhelmingly present and construct roles for mothers as agentic advocates in empowering ways.

An ancillary finding to both of these primary observations is that the tone of the public conversation was not particularly heated, nor was it divisive or polarized. There were no strong voices raised to counter the dominant discursive constructions of Rowan Stringer as a heroic athlete and her mother as a laudable advocate for safer sports. A further ancillary finding bears mentioning: I do not think that this study evidences an erosion of the discourse of mother-blame generally across Canadian society. Rather, mother-blame has a phantom presence in the media texts because advocates and authors clearly and expressly refute it. Rowan Stringer's case seems to be an instance in which the public narrative was successfully directed by advocates. Her mother, and other mothers in their community, anticipated, spoke back to, and actively resisted widely accepted discourses of mother-blame.

Overwhelmingly, in the Stringer case, the deceased is referred to first and foremost as an athlete. The language of Rowan's Law and the inquest recommendations is gender neutral. They talk about "youth," "children." and "sport," and address the needs of "athletes." In media articles, Stringer is overwhelmingly presented as an "athlete" much more often than she is described as a "girl," "woman," or an otherwise gendered subject. By the numbers, according to the Factiva database, the most used keywords in the coverage of Stringer's case in media articles are

Young, athletes, concussion, legislation, youth, sports, play sports, multiple concussions, head injuries, youth concussions, real, diapers, head injury, blockbuster movie

Even in traditionally conservative media publications, Stringer's death was portrayed overwhelmingly as a case of "youth concussions" among "athletes" who are "under pressure to power through and take one for the team" (V. Hall). Perhaps because the leading political proponent of law reform after Rowan Stringer's death was her own elected representative, Lisa McLeod, a woman, mother, and a conservative, Stringer's case was not the subject of heated public debate. Or perhaps timing mattered at least as much. Coverage of the Stringer inquest—which focused on concussions as a medical issue and linked the death of student athletes with deaths and injuries of professional athletes, such as football players—coincided with the release of the film *Concussion* and a growing public awareness of issues relating to concussions in sport.

Stringer in the media articles is characterized as an athlete. Gender is not the primary focus of how she is configured. Rather, the focus is on her experience and playing ability. She is called "one of the experienced players on the team" and "captain" (Payne). Descriptors of her in news coverage are often gender neutral such as "Ottawa teen" (Payne). Stringer is also identified as a "youth athlete" "youth" or "player" (Baines). However, it would be over simplistic to say that gender is irrelevant to the Stringer case. Discursive figures of girl-Rowan or child-Rowan are present within, and strategically claimed in, the texts, but they never dominate them. Stringer is not primarily constructed as a gendered subject, but rather as an athlete. Her role in sport has provided for her an identity that transcends and even seems to transform gendering processes in her case. There is a consistent use in the coverage of genderless descriptors that evidences intentionality. It is clear that deliberate and active resistance against stereotypical ideas about girls and sport was engaged in on the part of journalists, legal actors, and Rowan's parents, against prevailing norms and narratives of gender.

The word "girl" does appear as an identifier for Rowan Stringer in the coverage, but infrequently, and seldom does the phrase "girl athlete" or "female athlete" appear (V. Hall). At the beginning of one article, which is an in-depth "special investigation," Stringer is called a "17-year-old rugby player," and it is only much later in the piece that she is referenced as "Rowan Stringer, a 17-year-old Ottawa girl" (V. Hall). Here, unusually among the coverage, Stringer is described primarily as a "young woman" and a "girl" as opposed to focusing on her role as an athlete. She is described as a "talented caregiver," and the piece opens up with a description of her, as a child, devotedly taking care of her dolls. However, this nurturing capability is not contrasted with but rather legitimizes her athlete identity and configuration in the article. Some include "Girl, 17, died after two head injuries in less than a week" (19 May 2015). Note that here, where she is identified as a girl in the headline, she is not identified as an athlete. Later in the article, she is referred to as a warrior and teen in the following sentence: "the teen called her injuries 'warrior wounds' and wore them with pride."

This identification of Stringer as a "warrior" is of a genderless subject, a "teen." She is also called an "Ottawa teenager" (Keith). As a rugby player, Stringer is permitted somehow in the text to be a warrior, and athlete, and also a girl.

In the media stories, in the inquest testimony, and in the political debates about law reform, actors self-identifying as mothers were the leading speaking subjects in all texts. The key actors involved were Stringer's mother and the local MPP Lisa McLeod of the Progressive Conservative Party in Ontario, who is also a mother. In the texts, McLeod frequently invokes her own role as a mother in her advocacy toward better measures to be taken regarding concussions and sports in Ontario schools. It is by occupying and invoking the social location of mother and appealing to other mothers and fathers and their concern for children that both Rowan's own mother Kathleen Stringer and MPP Lisa McLeod have spoken in the case of Rowan's death. Kathleen Stringer has been actively fighting for schools to address concussion management while retaining sport programs. At the inquest, Kathleen Stringer received significant media attention for vowing the death of a young athlete in these circumstances should "never happen again"(Cobb).

The Rowan Stringer case as a matter of public conversation presents a promising example of how women's sport and mothers' activism can provide spaces for actors to resist familiar and oppressive tropes of mother-blame and lead change toward more egalitarian gender relations. In glaring contrast to my prior study of Ashley Smith's inquest, in which her subjectivity as an agent was fundamentally undermined by the insistence on acceptance of her configuration as a victim, mental patient, and feminine girl (Bromwich), Stringer's agency was made visible and supported in the case around her death. Although the cases are not simple opposites, and there are complex differences between the deaths of these two Canadian teen girls, this contrast does provide evidence for the claim that when girls are understood as athletes, it provides a window into seeing them as complex, agentic people. Equally, mothers who promote their children's athleticism walk a fine line between being seen as good mothers and a variety of figures of the bad mother.

The case of the Stringer inquest is a revealing instance of sport as a site of resistance to patriarchal discourses and relations. Analysis of how Stringer is talked about in her case reveals how performances of athleticism by women and girls can disrupt gendered ideologies, and how participation in sport can dislodge assumptions about the gendered body. Athleticism by girls appears, on this analysis, to provide movement toward the construction of "ungendered" human athletes, and affords potential for mothers, girls, and women to recreate ourselves and our society. Whereas gender logic has been disrupted by the participation of high school girls in women's rugby, it appears that the logics of mother-blame have been disrupted as well.

The public case arising from Rowan Stringer's death is an inspiring narrative of community unity forging positive change from tragedy, which makes significant movement toward better education about, and treatment of, concussions acquired while playing sport. At the same time, the case contributes to the advancement of women, girls, and mothers. Advocates should take note: agentic portrayals of girls and women are powerful tools for advancement of equality just as passive portrayals can have troubling results. How girls and women are configured in discourse affects material outcomes in their lives, and we should be mindful of how this is done.

Conclusion

Rowan Stringer, a heroic figure in death as in life, brought home a remarkable win in law reform for other young athletes. Her death resulted in the ushering in of a new province-wide regime for dealing with youth concussions, the first law of its kind in Canada. The critical discourse analysis presented in this chapter reveals how in the case of Rowan Stringer's death, led by agentic, socially powerful mothers, a community came together to find better ways to address athlete concussions in sport. Although Stringer died while playing a nontraditional women's sport, and a backlash against women in sport was expected, the spectres of misogyny and mother-blame are actively resisted in the coverage of, and legal consideration given to, her case.

Critical discourse analysis of texts produced in the Rowan Stringer case reveals that mothers are actively engaged in working to make change from the legacy of Stringer's death, and they invoked their maternal roles in doing so. Perhaps this means that feminist theorization about women's sport and women's rugby in particular can have community-building functions as spaces to challenge hegemonic masculinities, misogynies, and oppressive understandings of bad mothering is confirmed by this study. However, it may also be that mothers' longstanding role as regulators of children's health and wellbeing is what is being invoked and performed here and that the deployment of maternal subjectivities in advocacy and law reform is something less revolutionary than has been suggested here.

However, absent from the texts comprising the case are more complex feminist critiques of the performativity of violent sports as linked to hypermasculinity. Even in the face of the significant legal win for mothers, girls, children, and athletes, I have lingering concerns. A nagging worry for me in being a mother of girls and a boy who play sports is if rough sports such as rugby are opportunities to perform violent masculinity, the transgressive act of women and girls participating in these same sports may afford them opportunities to transgress gender norms and disrupt gender logic, but their participation could simultaneously replicate violence as a performance of power.

In the public case of Rowan Stringer's death, and in the statutory language of Rowan's Law, the content of what constitutes a sport as a valuable social and community activity is not questioned. The concerted discursive embrace of Stringer as an athlete here, although it is empowering, is not unambiguously something with which I am comfortable because she died by socially sanctioned violence, even as her friends and loved ones cheered from the sidelines. Indeed, her commitment to denying her injuries and playing through pain, which the inquest found contributed to her death, is consistent with problematic aspects of violent masculinity that deny feelings and vulnerabilities. By foregrounding and celebrating Stringer as an athlete playing a valorized game, texts comprising the case have accepted, even defended, the rules and roughness of rugby as a given.

If certain contact sports are problematic as performances of violent masculinity, which are dangerous to their players, are they not still problematic even if it is subjects gendered female actually doing the performance? On the one hand, if a sport exists and is a locus for the performance and attainment of skills, experience, and power, then all should be able to participate in it without discrimination, equally. In sports where the athletic and social games being performed involve violence, and seem to indicate the powerful operation of mandates to achieve self-destructive and hypermasculinity, it may be that the game should be reformulated too. Likely because of the concerted effort on the part of advocates to resist notions that girls or women are unsuited to sports, there has been a completely uncritical acceptance of rugby.

Although there have been changes in broader Canadian society to how violence is treated in other sports, such as hockey, over the last fifteen years, a question I have not seen asked in the Stringer case is whether the sport of rugby could be played with less violence, especially when the players are children or adolescents. Even though sports provide potential for allowing women and girls new roles in larger social games, attention should be paid to the question of whether those games need changing. If we take seriously sports' power to, as Mandela says, "change the world," we should consider ways to change sports and to recognize other fields of human endeavour that are less ablest, gendered, and violent, as places where courage and agency can be developed and displayed.

Works Cited

Berlant, Lauren. "On the Case." *Critical Inquiry*, vol. 33, no. 4, 2007, pp. 663-72.

Bill 149, *Rowan's Law Advisory Committee Act*, 2016.

Bromwich, Rebecca. *Looking for Ashley: What the Smith Case Reveals about the Government of Girls, Mothers, and Families in Canada*. Demeter Press, 2015.

Bryson, L. "Sport and the Maintenance of Masculine Hegemony." *Women, Sport and Culture*, edited by C. Cole, Human Kinetics, 1994, pp. 31-46.

Caplan, Paula J. "Mother Blame." *Encyclopedia of Motherhood*. SAGE Publications, 2010.

Carlin, John. *Playing the Enemy: Nelson Mandela and the Game That Made a Nation*. Penguin Press, 2008.

Castañeda, Claudia. *Figurations: Child, Bodies, Worlds*. Duke University Press, 2002.

Coakley, J. *Sport and Society*. McGraw Hill, 2001.

Cobb, Chris, "Never Again, Mother Vows at Rowan Stringer Concussion Inquest" *Ottawa Citizen* (20 May 2015).

De Lauretis, Teresa. *Figures of Resistance: Essays in Feminist Theory*. University of Illinois Press, 2007.

Hall, M. A. *Feminism and Sporting Bodies*. Human Kinetics, 1996.

Hall, M. Ann. "Knowledge and Gender: Epistemological Questions in the Social Analysis of Sport." *Sociology of Sport Journal*, vol. 2, no. 1, 1985, pp. 25-42.

Hall, Vicky. "Rowan's Law." *National Post*, 2015https://nationalpost.com/features/rowans-law, Accessed 30 May 2016.

Johnson, Rebecca. *Taxing Choices: The Intersection of Class, Gender, Parenthood and the Law*. University of British Columbia Press, 2002.

Johnstone, Hillary. "Rowan's Pitch Dedicated to Memory of Young Rugby Player." CBC News, 4 June 2016, www.cbc.ca/news/canada/ottawa/rowan-stringer-rugby-field-1.3616778. Accessed 19 June 2018.

Light, Richard, and David Kirk. "High School Rugby, the Body, and the Reproduction of Hegemonic Masculinity." *Sport, Education and Society*, vol. 5, no. 2, 2000, pp. 163-76.

Obituary of Rowan Stringer, *Ottawa Citizen* 16 May 2016.

O'Hanley, John Arthur. *Women in Non-Traditional Sport: The Rise and Popularity of Women's Rugby in Canada*. MA Thesis, Queen's University, 1998.

Payne, Elizabeth. "Ottawa Teen Died of Second Impact Syndrome" *Ottawa Citizen*, 16 June 2014, ottawacitizen.com/news/local-news/ottawa-teen-athlete-died-of-second-impact-syndrome. Accessed 19 June 2018.

Pringle, R. "Competing discourses: Narratives of a Fragmented Self, Manliness and Rugby Union." *International Review for the Sociology of Sport*, vol. 36, no. 4, 2001, pp. 425-39.

Reimer, Vanessa, and Sahagian, Sarah, *The Mother-Blame Game*. Demeter Press, 2015.

Schacht, S. P. "Misogyny On and Off the 'Pitch': The Gendered World of Male Rugby Players." *Gender & Society*, vol. 10, no. 5, 1996, pp. 550-65.

Scrogum, Jeanine. *M.S. Binaries and Bridging: A Feminist Analysis of Women's Rugby Participation*. MA Thesis, University of North Carolina, 2005.

Verdict of Coroner's Jury, RE: The Death of Rowan Stringer. *Ontario Office of the Chief Coroner*, 3 June 2015, www.mcscs.jus.gov.on.ca/english/Deathinvestigations/Inquests/Verdictsandrecommendations/OCCInquestStringer2015.html. Accessed 5 July 2018.

Wood, J. C. E. "Discovering the Ontario Inquest." *Osgoode Hall Law Journal*, vol. 5, no. 2, 1967, pp. 243-66.

Chapter 6

Sports, Moms, School, and Stress: My Story

Helaina Bromwich, Age Twelve

I do competitive gymnastics, and it costs a lot of money. In my family, everyone does at least one sport, and it is what we do. But when my mom was little, she was not allowed to play sports because her mom said she couldn't because she was a girl, but her dad convinced her mom to let her do life guarding. The hard thing for parents and sports is the driving or at least that is what my mom says. She says that she is always driving back and forth to school and back to gymnastics and back. Though I don't often tell her I am grateful that she takes the time to drive me places and that she lets me do what I love. On the other hand, sports are tough on kids as well; if you do a lot of sports, it is hard to get schoolwork done on time.

A lot of kids think that it is unfair that we have homework, since we go to school for five out of seven days. I am not saying that I don't agree with this opinion or that I do, only that it is a valid point. Sometimes, so much stress is put on us children that we forget we go to school to learn. Time pressure pushes us to prioritize quantity over quality of activities. The other day, one of my friends said, "I don't care if I get this right; I just want to be done." Often, this is how kids feel, and they forget that they are supposed to learn during school.

Stress can be caused because when a teacher says that something is for homework for the next day, and everyone becomes stressed because they have an activity or a sport that night, so they can't finish their work. It can put stress on children and then maybe when they go home, they will act angry at their parents when they are really angry at their professor or just generally mad about getting extra homework.

Moms will often get upset or overtired because their children act mad at them and then when the child goes to school, the teacher will be upset that the homework is not done then act that out on their students. It is a cycle that is completely avoidable. All of this causes stress to everyone—if you are the teacher, the child, the parent, or the teacher's child. My mother often gets upset for this reason. She says that many of her students slack off and don't do their homework. This is proof that this cycle does happen but if it's not the fault of the teacher, parent, child, or sports then how can we avoid this situation?

Notes on Contributors

Judy E. Battaglia is a clinical professor of communication studies at Loyola Marymount University in Los Angeles where she teaches classes in rhetorical methodology and criticism, gender communication, sports communication and theatre. She is also a primary faculty advisor. Her research interests include but are not limited to performance theory, poststructuralist analysis, feminist theory, close-textual analysis, pop culture, psychoanalysis, cultural studies, and critical biography. She has published several academic pieces on motherhood.

Helaina Bromwich was twelve years old when her contribution in this volume was written. She is now a high school student. In addition to pursuing international baccalaureate studies, and studying piano and voice, she competes in gymnastics at the Ontario provincial level and also runs track and cross country. She enjoys reading, writing, sailing, and swimming as well as gymnastics, and spending time with her friends.

Rebecca Bromwich is a mom to four kids in competitive sports. She is also a lawyer, legal academic, and activist. She lives in Ottawa, Ontario, where she is a faculty member at Carleton University's Department of Law and Legal Studies, and serves as an assistant crown attorney. Rebecca has co-edited and authored several Demeter Press collections and a monograph, as well as legal textbooks.

Catherine Ma is an associate professor of psychology in the behavioural sciences and human services department at Kingsborough Community College. Her love of psychology trumped being an accountant when she first took introduction to psychology at Baruch College. She later transferred to The University at Albany where she met the love of her life and received her bachelor's degree in psychology. As she continued to pursue her love of psychology, she earned her master's degree in psychology from Hunter College while working as the assistant undergraduate psychology advisor. Her thesis advisor planted the seeds of further graduate study and she earned her master's degree in philosophy and doctoral degree in social-personality psychology at the Graduate Center of CUNY.

Celeste Orr received their PhD from the Institute of Feminist and Gender Studies at the University of Ottawa. Celeste is currently an Adjunct Professor of Gender and Sexuality Studies at St. Lawrence University. Celeste's areas of research include the intersection of intersex and disability, body-mind diversity, sexuality and queer theories, and LGBTQI+ rights.

Kindell Foley Peters is a Ph.D. candidate in Educational Psychology at Oklahoma State University. This work is part of a larger doctoral dissertation, Women's Coaching Experiences: Oral Histories of Coaching, Gender, and Pedagogy, under the direction of Lucy Bailey, Ph.D., Oklahoma State University.

Pamela Morgan Redela is a mother of two, a wife, and friend to many feminist co-conspirators. She holds a BA, MA, and PhD in Spanish Language, Literature, and Culture, and teaches in the Women's Studies Department of California State University, San Marcos. Her research focuses on gender roles and feminist activism, ecofeminism, and intersectional feminist analysis of women's issues globally. Her writings have been published in *Ms. Magazine* (Winter, 2011) and the Demeter Press anthologies *Feminist Parenting* (2016) and *Stay-at-Home Mothers: Dialogues and Debates* (2014).

Amanda Watson received her PhD from the Institute of Feminist and Gender Studies at the University of Ottawa. She is interested in critical pedagogy for university teaching, with a focus on how to interrogate issues of social justice and power in the classroom. Her research examines the intersections of gendered and racialized citizenship, labour responsibility, paid and unpaid care work, maternal affect, and human and social reproduction. Her most recent publications explore the maternal responsibility to generate good feelings in others.